roaring lambs

roaring lambs

a gentle plan to
radically change
your world

Bob Briner

ZondervanPublishingHouse
Grand Rapids, Michigan

A Division of HarperCollins*Publishers*

Roaring Lambs
Copyright © 1993 by Bob Briner
Foreword copyright © 2000 by Bob Briner

Requests for information should be addressed to:

📖 ZondervanPublishingHouse
Grand Rapids, Michigan 49530

Library of Congress Cataloging-in-Publication Data

Briner, Bob.
    Roaring Lambs : a gentle plan to radically change your world / Bob
Briner.
       p.   cm.
    ISBN 0-310-59111-2 (softcover)
    1. Church and the world 2. Christian life—1960 3. Christianity and the
arts—United States. 4. Christianity and culture. I. Title.
BR115. W6873
261'.1—dc20   99-41265

Interior design by Laura Klynstra Blost

Printed in the United States of America

00 01 02 03 04 05 06 /❖ DC/ 17 16 15 14 13 12 11 10 9

*For Rob, Leigh, and Lynn
and especially for Marty
who inspire me to attempt good things*

contents

acknowledgments

As a first-time author of a book, I feel a deep sense of debt and gratitude to those whose help was given so effectively and generously.

The people at Zondervan could not have provided better or more gracious help and support. Publisher Scott Bolinder has been a constant source of encouragement. My editor Lyn Cryderman, has contributed helpful guidance as well. By the way, both of these guys must assume full responsibility for the title, *Roaring Lambs*. I wanted *Saline Solution*. Get it? Briner—salt— saline? Okay, maybe they were right.

Edwin Pope, the brilliant sports editor of the Miami Herald and my friend read and commented on the manuscript as it was being written. His suggestions have been invaluable.

Dr. Ray Pritchard, senior pastor of Calvary Memorial Church in Oak Park, Illinois, provided his considerable expertise in the area of Scripture and theology. Any shortcomings in these areas are mine, not his. He also directly inspired several approaches the book pursues. I am very grateful to him.

Many of the experiences that gave me the insights for this book were enjoyed in the company of Donald Dell, my partner and friend for over twenty years. We have traveled together from Toledo to Tashkent and from Dayton to Dubai. My thanks for many things.

My faithful secretary, Mary Ann Milazzotto, typed the entire manuscript and was also a source of encouragement along the way. Rebecca Bowman, also in the ProServe Television office, assisted Mary Ann. My thanks to both of them.

—*RAB Dallas, Texas*

Take the following test by answering each statement yes or no, then check your score at the end.

1. I have attended a school board meeting within the last year.
2. I have as many close friends outside the church as within.
3. I own at least one original piece of art.
4. In the last year I have written a letter of praise to a network or sponsor of a television program.
5. I support decent movies by attending wholesome ones and avoiding unwholesome ones.
6. I consider careers in the arts, journalism, literature, film, and television to be as important for the kingdom as pastoral ministry, or foreign missions.
7. I have written at least one letter to the editor of my local newspaper in the last year.
8. I have read at least on book on the New York Times Bestseller List in the past year.
9. I am active in the civic affairs of my community.
10. I have talked with at least one non-Christian about my relationship with Christ and what it means to be His follower

If you answered yes to:

8–10   A bona fide Roaring Lamb!
5–7   Watch out, they're starting to listen.
2–4   Mouth open, no sound.
0-1   B-a-a-a-a-a-a-a-a-a-a

Bob Briner was a good friend of mine, and I consider him one of my mentors. The philosophy of *Roaring Lambs* is one I have made my own for a long time. I have tried to convey to people that we can live out our faith much more powerfully if we would talk less and live more.

Imagine a world full of world-class entertainers, movie directors, screenwriters, Broadway actors, journalists, and painters, all of whom have a passionate devotion to Christ. What's more, think of those people being recognized and respected in their professional worlds and in the broader culture, and the opportunities they would have to shout the good news of God's grace with the power of their lives, without a word being spoken. It would impact our culture more dramatically than we could imagine.

Roaring Lambs is a wake-up call from Bob to the church that he loved so dearly. It is a call from a man who lived the book's premise far beyond anyone's comprehension, and who wished passionately for more people to take God's call to shape the culture from within; to be salt and light—illuminating, flavoring, and preserving our culture's creative community with the good news of God's grace and redemption.

Roaring Lambs is as powerful today as it was groundbreaking in its first year of publication. Bob's fear that the church had abdicated its role as a force to shape modern culture is being realized more fully by the day. And yet Bob did not wish that the church would shrink from its place in culture. Instead, he challenged committed believers to run headlong into the culture with excellence, integrity, and conviction. He challenges us still to not just shape culture, but to earn the right to roar in a community that has been ostracized from much of the church for far too long.

I miss Bob. And yet I know his legacy lives on in the hearts and actions of people who impact our culture by being a part of it: bands in clubs, singers on the radio, actors, directors, and journalists who pursue their craft with excellence—all giving credit to God's gifts and adopting the charge of St. Francis of Assisi, to "preach the Gospel at all times, and, if necessary, use words."

—Michael W. Smith

preface

The Shah of Iran had summoned me to meet with him during his international tennis tournament at the sprawling Imperial Country Club on the outskirts of Tehran. As I stood beside the U.S. ambassador awaiting the imminent arrival of the Shah and the Empress, one question continually came to mind: "What am I doing here?"

The same question occurred to me as I was flying over on Air Iran, one of the world's most luxurious airlines in the pre-Ayatollah days. Mike Wallace of *60 Minutes* was on the flight on his way to interview the Shah, and we chatted about tennis, but mostly I kept pondering the question, "What am I doing here?"

This same question had presented itself often in the past. It came as I stood on the sidelines at Shea Stadium as a part of the Miami Dolphins' front office staff before our game with the New York Jets. As I sat in the Royal Box at Wimbledon, it came to mind again. The same question arose as I rode with Akio Morita, the legendary founder of Sony, in his limousine through the streets of Tokyo. When the U.S. ambassador to Australia sent his plane to Sydney to fly a small group of us to the embassy in Canberra, I asked myself that question. And it certainly floated in and out of my mind when tennis great Jack Kramer and I entered the magnificent suite atop Caesars Palace in Las Vegas to negotiate with the hard men who ran the gambling empire. "What am I doing here?" "Why am I here?"

Naturally, everyone asks this question from time to time, but coming as I did from humble beginnings—the product of a modest public school system and two very small colleges, it seemed

totally preposterous that I should be flying all over the world, hob-
nobbing with the rich and famous, unless there was something
more to life than just fate and chance. For me, the question "What
am I doing here?" was more complex and urgent because of one
fact. I am a Christian. I am committed to the cause of Christ. I
want to serve Him. So what am I doing here? What am I doing on
this jet to Paris where I will oversee television production for the
great bicycle race, the Tour de France? Why am I doing what I do
instead of pastoring a church or training missionaries?

As career opportunities took me from coaching six-man football at a tiny high school on the plains of Kansas to some of the
most powerful positions in international sports and sports television, I found myself much better prepared to succeed both professionally and socially than I was prepared to succeed as an
effective Christian. Even trying to live a life that integrated the
Bible with all I was doing, I found myself progressing much more
rapidly professionally and socially than spiritually—particularly
in doing Christianity, in fulfilling the commands of Christ, in
being salt in the world. As I look back it is easy to understand why
this was so. Both in business and social settings, I had many mentors and role models, many patterns to follow. Many people were
there to teach me and help me. On the other hand, the more I
progressed in my sports business career, the more isolated and
alone I felt as a Christian. Spiritually, I was a meek and lowly lamb
in a world full of lions. The *real* Christians were people like my
pastor, people working full-time for Campus Crusade, Youth for
Christ, or Wheaton College, the countless missionaries sent out
by my church, Billy Graham, Charles Stanley, Jerry Falwell, James
Dobson. These were the ones changing the world. The best I
could hope for was to support them in prayer and money.

At least that's what I had been taught.

The wonderful people who had attracted me to a very small, very conservative church in Dallas, Texas, and who introduced me to the marvelous reality of a personal relationship with Jesus Christ seemed to be both intimidated by and skeptical about one of their own venturing out into the world of big-time professional sports. This just didn't square with their previous experiences. The emphasis in my church was on personal piety and separation from the world. The Miami Dolphins and network television seemed light years away from the small sanctuary in South Dallas. As I searched for help in combining Christian living with my world of professional sports and television, it didn't come from my church or denomination. And in fairness to this great group of believers, I have not found much help in this area from any of the other traditional evangelical groups.

At two small Christian colleges affiliated with the same denomination as that of my home church, I spent four wonderful years, received a high-quality education, and was further grounded in my commitment to the Christian faith. I made many wonderful friends and met a lovely young woman who became my wife. That, by itself, is a tremendous contribution, but in my opinion, my preparation to go out into the real world and live my faith effectively was lacking. Already planning on a career in sports management, I felt I was a sort of second-class campus citizen. My classmates who were preparing for the pulpit ministry or missionary service were the ones who were treated as if they would be doing the real work of the church. The rest of us were the supporting cast.

Almost nothing in my church or collegiate experiences presented possibilities for a dynamic, involved Christian life outside the professional ministry. If you were called to "full-time Christian service," there were very clear paths to follow. If not, you were pretty much on your own. You heard about being salt and light, but no one told you how to do it, other than to get involved in a good local church.

I have since learned that my experiences are far from unique. I have met countless Christian lay men and women who also feel as if their professional careers are to be set aside in that category as "secular," while their faith is relegated to the church. "Professional" Christians in full-time service do the real ministry of the church, while we follow along, not really sure what we are doing here.

At first, I was somewhat relieved to learn I wasn't the only one to feel as if I had blown it by not going into full-time Christian service, but then I began to feel even worse. What a shame that so many of us feel sort of in a fog between our faith and our careers. I am convinced that most Christians have no idea about the possibilities of being lambs that roar—of being followers of God who know how to fully integrate their commitment to Christ into their daily lives. Maybe that's why so many areas of modern life so clearly lack the preserving salt of the Gospel.

My agent, Sealy Yates, provides yet another example of how the church has somehow missed the mark. A leading literary and entertainment attorney in Southern California, Sealy grew up in rural Southern Baptist churches in West Texas. He heard and responded to the clear, beautiful call of the Gospel and went on to attend Baylor University, which at that time was one of the country's leading Christian institutions of higher education. After graduating from Baylor he went on to get a law degree at UCLA.

Here was Sealy's situation: He was a strongly committed Christian, was able to attend a major university where God's Word was honored, became the first member of his family to obtain a college degree, had earned a law degree from a prestigious law school, had married the girl of his dreams, had entered into a promising law practice, had a new baby boy, was teaching a Sunday school class in a Bible-believing church, and was extremely miserable! It would seem he had it all, but, in Sealy's mind, if what he had was all there was, it was far from enough.

In all those years in Southern Baptist churches, in four years at Baylor, in attending and working in a great Los Angeles area church, no one had ever told Sealy how he could make the dynamic of the Gospel reach into all areas of his life. Once he decided the professional ministry was not his calling, he pretty much resigned himself to being a compartmentalized Christian, an idea that seemed to be supported by the church. His profession was in one box, his life for Christ in the church in another. For Sealy, this type of Christian life was frustrating and discouraging.

Through God's grace, Sealy was not left in his misery. A small poster on the church bulletin board caught his eye. It said, "Come! Learn how to share your faith and live the abundant life Christ promised." With some skepticism but also with hope and excitement, he and his wife Susan attended these meetings sponsored by Campus Crusade for Christ, and for the first time he was told how he could live a fully integrated life, could make his profession as much a part of his service to God as his church activities, could obey the scriptural admonition to be salt in the world—could become a roaring lamb!

Sealy Yates now heads a successful law firm and literary agency. He serves both Christian and non-Christian clients but represents them all through a practice based on Christian principles. The contracts drawn by his firm cite scriptural imperatives. The opportunities to witness for Christ abound. The opportunities to help others proclaim the Gospel through their talents are there in great numbers.

In a profession not blessed these days with a sterling reputation, Sealy in many ways personifies what it means to be a roaring lamb. He will not single-handedly change the legal profession, but he will be an influence for good with all those he contacts. The leaders of the American Bar Association may never even know about him, but many will know more about his Lord because of the way he practices law. He is obeying Christ's command to be salt in the world. He shows on a daily basis, in the rough and tumble of an inherently contentious profession, that Christ is real and relevant, that His plan works. Anyone who has been represented by Sealy, or anyone who has opposed him in negotiation or litigation can testify to the fact that he is no namby-pamby. He is a strong, tough advocate and thoroughly professional. The difference is that his practice conforms not only to the rules of the California Bar but also, and more particularly, to the rules contained in God's Word.

Through all those years Sealy Yates grew up in the church, attended college and graduate school, was married, became a father, and was out in his profession before ever hearing anything practical and enabling about being salt in the world. It was pretty much the same for me. Plus, once I left the expected career path of college teaching and coaching to become a professional sports executive, I felt cut off, isolated and alone as a Christian.

I was taught how to be a lamb, but I was never taught to roar.

I'm writing this book because I think it's time for more lambs to roar. It's time for believers to confidently carry their faith with them into the marketplace so that our very culture feels the difference. I'm writing to parents and ministry professionals with the prayerful hope that they will begin more intensely and systematically to teach and model the reality that every one of us is called to be a minister in our own corner of the world. I am writing with the hope that the dichotomy between professional Christians and Christians in the professions will be greatly lessened. I am writing with the hope that every reader will better understand how to carry out the scriptural admonition to be salt in a world that so desperately needs that preservative. And I am writing with the hope that Christian young people will choose careers and professions that will place them in the "culture shaping" venues of our world.

I don't pretend to have all the answers, but I'm beginning to learn from my own mistakes as well as the well-intentioned errors of my friends in the church. During the almost thirty years I have spent in professional football, professional basketball, professional tennis, and television production I have produced thousands of hours of television programming and written for such publications as the *New York Times, Sports Illustrated,* and the *Miami Herald,* to list only a few. My travels have taken me all over the globe, and I have developed wonderful friendships with the wealthy and well-known (being neither myself). Unfortunately, this book will recount more of opportunities missed than of opportunities taken. But I hope that even that will help you to take better advantage of your own daily opportunities to obey Christ's command to be salt and light in the world. I hope it will help you answer the question "What am I doing here?" with steadfast assurance. My prayer is that this book will be the beginning of a transformation in your own life that will help you become a roaring lamb.

God bless you.

—Bob Briner, Dallas, Texas 1992

introduction
don't try this alone

You will see almost immediately that this is a book about doing, about action, about making things happen. It is about retaking lost territory, about winning, about conquest. But it is also a book in which I try very hard to base everything I say on biblical principles. And one of the most overriding and compelling principles of the Bible is the truth that in our own strength we can do nothing. Unless we have waited on the Lord in prayer and received His direction and blessing, what we do will be ineffective and futile.

As he usually does, author and pastor Chuck Swindoll has a good word for us in this regard. In a compelling sermon on Joshua and the walls of Jericho, Pastor Swindoll emphasizes the axiom "Consecration precedes conquest." Before we can win, we must have committed our course of action to God. To consecrate means to set apart. We must put our own desires, goals, motives, and plans aside in favor of God's direction. And to know His direction for us, we must devote ourselves to prayer and to the Word.

A good and wise friend recently pointed out to me the paramount role prayer played in the miraculous successes of the early church as recorded in the book of Acts. The key passage, one we often move past very quickly, is "These with one mind were continually devoting themselves to prayer" (Acts 1:14NAS). As my friend said, the first thing the disciples did after Christ ascended into heaven was to devote themselves to prayer—not evangelism, healing, or preaching, but prayer. This became their pattern. Just consider all the references to prayer in Acts:

    1:24   Then they prayed

2:42   They devoted themselves to . . . prayer
4:24   . . . raised their voices together in prayer
4:31   After they prayed
6:4   . . . will give our attention to prayer
7:59   Stephen prayed . . .
8:15   . . . they prayed for them
9:11   . . . for he is praying
10:9   Peter went up on the roof to pray
10:30 . . . I was in my house praying
12:5   . . . but the church was earnestly praying
12:12 . . . many people had gathered and were praying
13:3   So after they had fasted and prayed
14:23 . . . and, with prayer and fasting, committed them
       to the Lord
16:13 . . . to find a place of prayer
16:16 . . . going to the place of prayer
16:25 About midnight Paul and Silas were praying
20:36 . . . he knelt down with all of them and prayed
28:8   . . . after prayer

Prayer dominates the book of Acts!

So before *you* act, you must pray. The only way we can really change the world is to immerse our wills and desires so completely in the mind of Christ that we become extensions of His ministry to mankind. The best way to do that is to pray.

If our ambition is political (get the right party in office), social (create more compassionate structures), moral (clean up a sin-sick culture), or even "spiritual" (build bigger and more attractive churches and programs), we will surely fail. Instead, our ambition to become roaring lambs is to more completely serve and obey our Lord who has asked us to be salt and light. If we are not in a right relationship to Him, our own ambitions will get in the way.

So begin this journey on your knees. I will be asking you (as I continue to ask myself) to break out of the comfortable world you have created and stride boldly into the coliseum. To roar back at the lions, not in a fight to devour and destroy them, but with the voice of Christ who brings good news to all.

Don't try this alone. You'll never make it. You can become a roaring lamb only through the power and strength of the Master. May He be with you as you roar out into the darkness, bringing the light of the Gospel.

> Then Pharoh said to Joseph, "Since God has made all this known to you, there is no one so discerning and wise as you. You shall be in charge of my palace and all my people are to submit to your orders."
>
> Genesis 41:39–40

1

Clear Your Throats, It's Time to Roar

Let's face it. Despite the fact that roughly 80 percent of Americans claim to believe in Jesus as the Son of God, we're not doing so hot. Collectively, as the church of Jesus Christ—the church against which the gates of hell shall not prevail—we're struggling.

I can almost hear the chorus of defense. What do you mean we're struggling! Church attendance is at its highest in decades. Look at all the big, active churches we've built. Consider the tremendous contributions of Christian television—networks that span the globe with the message of the Gospel. And what about the church-based antiabortion victories? Why, we've gotten so strong that the president listens to us on this and other issues.

The chorus continues.

Look at all the truly Christian colleges and universities that are turning out graduates who go into the world with the Gospel. And what about the Christian publishing industry? Why, almost every community has a Christian bookstore where people can buy Bibles and helpful Christian literature.

Okay, Bob, things might not be perfect, but don't blame the church.

Well, things are not even close to being perfect and to a certain extent, I do blame the church. For despite all the fancy buildings, sophisticated programs, and highly visible presence, it is my contention that the church is almost a nonentity when it comes to shaping culture. In the arts, entertainment, media, education, and other culture-shaping venues of our country, the church has abdicated its role as salt and light.

Culturally, we are lambs. Meek, lowly, easily dismissed cuddly creatures that are fun to watch but never a threat to the status quo.

It's time for those lambs to roar.

Remember the movie *Network*? There was a poignant scene where the character played by Peter Finch encourages viewers of his nightly newscast to open their windows and shout out to no one in particular, "I'm mad as h—, and I'm not going to take it anymore."

Well, I'm more sad than mad, but as the corporate body of the Prince of Peace and King of Kings, we don't have to take it anymore.

We don't need to take the rap that we're just a bunch of do-gooders who need to be placated now and then by highly publicized visits with the president or an occasional feature story in the local newspaper on one of our many conventions and crusades.

We don't need to take the palliatives from our leaders who tell us, "Don't expect too much" when we decide to get involved in positive, constructive ways in our communities.

We don't have to be satisfied with a half-page religion section once a week when in reality religion is so much more than an add-on feature to life.

We don't have to sit back and wring our hands at the way our culture is going down the drain.

We don't have to be content with a position on the sidelines when our Lord Himself has assigned us a starting role on the winning team.

My point is really quite simple. Look around you. Can you honestly say that Christian influence is felt in Hollywood? That a Christian presence is evident in the major art galleries and museums of our land? That when you turn on the television you are aware of an underlying foundation of Judeo-Christian values in that medium? That as you pick up the morning newspaper you see objective (not favorable, just objective) treatment of religion in your community? That when you browse through the best-sellers at the airport bookstores you will find even one novel written by an active, church-going, born-again Christian?

Do you honestly believe that our big churches and highly visible Christian leaders have brought about a movement that is taken seriously in this country?

We feel we are making a difference because we are so important to ourselves. We have created a phenomenal subculture with our own media, entertainment, educational system, and political hierarchy so that we have the sense that we're doing a lot. But what we've really done is create a ghetto that is easily dismissed by the rest of society. If you don't believe me, try this: Go into your office or place of business and ask how many of your colleagues understand the doctrine of inerrancy or know what the apostle Paul meant with the word *kephale* or whether the rapture will come before, after, or during the tribulation. Sound silly? Perhaps, but those are the issues we Christians are spending so much time and energy on. These things may be important to us (or at least to our leaders), but they aren't important to the rest of the world. Real people with real problems—your neighbors and mine—just don't care about the things we argue and fight about. What's more, they see us arguing and fighting and decide they don't need what we have.

I'm afraid many in the world view us as a flock of lambs grazing in the safe pastures surrounding our churches that have been designed to blend right in with the neighborhood landscape. We're good neighbors. We look like everyone else. And except for Sunday morning, we follow the same patterns of behavior as those who have little or no interest in religion. Our lives are divided into sections labeled religious and secular, and neither category seems to affect the other. Consequently, our religious views are not taken very seriously.

I have a number of friends in network television, the business community, newspaper journalism, and the arts, and I've learned two things about them. First, they have little to do with Christianity, but second, they are consumed by their pursuit of success. What this has told me is that if I want to reach them with the Gospel, the worst thing I could do is invite them to church or "witness" to them during a break in a board meeting. On the other hand, if I want to point them toward the Savior, I need to make sure my professional behavior is stellar. I need to make the best presentations, close the most successful deals, deliver the greatest product I possibly can. To them, my work is a reflection of who I am. It makes no difference to them if I'm a Christian, Buddhist, or atheist, as long as I'm competent. These people are not anti-Christian. They haven't blacklisted me from their business meetings or their social events once they learned I was a Christian. If anything, they are the most spiritually hungry people I've ever met, but unless the church encourages our involvement in these arenas, my friends in television will most likely remain hungry and the Gospel will continue to be absent from their boardrooms and brainstorming sessions.

We need to reclaim the territory, not in a triumphalistic sense but out of a strong conviction that this is where we belong. Our churches are growing. Our colleges are full. Subscriptions and sales are up at our magazine- and book-publishing companies. And our broadcast media continue to bring our own music and teaching into our homes. In short, our subculture is healthy. *It* doesn't need more attention. It's the *world* that needs help.

It's time for the lambs to roar.

What I'm calling for is a radically different way of thinking about our world. Instead of running from it, we need to rush into it. And instead of just hanging around the fringes of our culture, we need to be right smack dab in the middle of it.

Why not believe that one day the most critically acclaimed director in Hollywood could be an active Christian layman in his church? Why not hope that the Pulitzer Prize for investigative reporting could go to a Christian journalist on staff at a major daily newspaper? Is it really too much of a stretch to think that a major exhibit at the Museum of Modern Art could feature the works of an artist on staff at one of our fine Christian colleges? Am I out of my mind to suggest that your son or daughter could be the principle dancer for the Joffrey Ballet Company, leading a weekly Bible study for other dancers in what was once considered a profession that was morally bankrupt?

I don't think so. In fact, I believe it has been the pessimistic vision of the church that has prevented generations of young people from venturing out into the culture-shaping professions of our world. I've always wondered why we could be so quick to sacrifice our children to become missionaries but stand in the way of their becoming broadcast journalists, film and television actors, photographers, and painters. It's almost as if we believe God is strong enough to take care of his own only as long as they stay within the safety of the Christian ghetto. And yet, the Bible gives us countless examples of people like Joseph, who not only served as an advisor to the "president" of his day but also used that position to influence the entire land.

Can't we do that today? Shouldn't we be encouraging and equipping our sons and daughters to become Josephs too?

A friend of mine told me about a conversation he had with a member of his church. The two were talking about their frustration over their church's inability to have any impact on their community. It was a relatively small church—about 150 members—in an upscale suburban Midwest city. Included in the congregation were a leading surgeon, several business executives, a department head of a prestigious public school, as well as a number of lawyers, teachers, and sales reps. But, my friend observed, we're just sort of treading water. Things are getting worse in our community, families are breaking up, our kids aren't even accepting our faith, and we seem to waste so much time fighting with each other.

My friend then recalled the response of his fellow church member: "Don't you know, Jim, this is as good as it gets."

That church, like so many others, is filled with lambs who've lost their voice. Not only have they failed to penetrate their community with their values, they have come to accept their failure as inevitable.

I believe it's not only possible but absolutely necessary for Christians and Christian values to become a vital element in the overall moral and cultural discourse of our nation. Without our strategic involvement in the culture-shaping arenas of art, entertainment, the media, education, and the like, this nation simply cannot be the great and glorious society it once was. If we are to be obedient to our Lord's call to go into all the world, we will begin reentering the fields that we have fled.

Are you ready to roar?

"You are the salt of the earth . . . You are the light of the world."

Matthew 5:13a; 14a

2

Salt: Make Use of It

I have a friend who raises sheep. He says they're among the most misunderstood of farm animals. True, he says, they are meek. They need someone to follow, and if they don't have a thoughtful, caring shepherd, they generally get themselves into trouble. Bigtime trouble.

But, says my friend the sheep farmer, their trust in their shepherd is so strong that they will do anything to follow the guy. In fact, he says, they can be the bravest, most assertive creatures when they feel secure in the care of their shepherd.

That's the kind of lambs we ought to be. We have a Shepherd we can trust fully, so we really ought to be out there on the front lines of battle for the cause of the Gospel. The fact that we aren't has a lot to do with our understanding (or misunderstanding) of those oft-quoted words from Matthew 5:13: *You are the salt.*

To the average Christian, salt is something that comes in a blue box and hides on the shelf until it's needed. That's our first mistake, but don't be too hard on yourself. If you have spent more than twenty minutes in church, you have probably heard that you are the salt of the earth. And most of what you've heard has probably made you feel guilty about not doing enough stuff. Never mind the fact that if you were gifted as an artist, businessman, or civic leader, no one could quite tell you what stuff you ought to be doing. All you had to look up to were people "in ministry" who were "called" to full-time Christian service. You really want to be salt? Take an early retirement and go to Haiti as a missionary.

That's not necessarily being salt, if I may mix a metaphor, nor is it what's required to be a roaring lamb.

This "salt" Scripture is so familiar, so much a part of the evangelical vernacular that it has lost much of its power. It is heard so often and used so much even in everyday language that it's imperative has dissipated.

I don't know about you, but when I think of someone who exemplifies this verse, I think of a little old lady who's been a great prayer warrior or an older, congenial gentleman who has given a lot to the church. Nothing against little old ladies and kind elderly men, but I've never been able to relate to that kind of person. Maybe someday I'll be one of those grandfatherly old men who sits close to the front every Sunday morning at church, but in the meantime I've got a business to run. Can I be salt also? Can I sit across the table from the chairman of the Sony Corporation and still have an impact on the world for Jesus? To most people in twentieth-century America, someone who is "the salt of the earth" is someone who is a rather dull, plodding, conforming individual—a hard worker, maybe, and honest but pretty tame, a loyal churchman who seldom does anything outside of church.

However, the salt Jesus has in mind is stinging, biting, cleansing, and preserving and is anything but dull, anything but tame.

To be the kind of salt Christ spoke about is to be on the cutting edge, in the fray, at the forefront of battle.

When Jesus said, "You are the salt of the earth," He was speaking to anyone then or now who accepts Him as Savior. It is one of the clearest declarations in Scripture from Jesus to His followers. Notice, He did not say for us to become salt. He said we are salt. Once we accept Him into our lives we automatically are the salt of the earth.

The second part of the verse gives us insight into what being salt should mean: "But if the salt loses its saltiness, how can it be made salty again? It is no longer good for anything, except to be thrown out and trampled by men." So, just being salt is not enough. In fact, if we are salt and are not being salty, isn't it fair to say that we are good-for-nothing Christians? That's what the Scripture says to me.

But the question is what do we *do*? How do we act as salt in our world? The answer lies in the way salt is used. Salt is both a seasoning and a preservative. It seasons by adding taste and enhancing flavor. It preserves by cleansing and retarding spoilage. In both cases, the salt must be brought in contact with is object for its power to be realized. Sitting in the shaker, it does no good. It might just as well be thrown out.

More than twenty years ago E. Stanley Jones, the great Methodist writer and missionary, was asked to name the number-one problem in the church. His quick reply was "Irrelevance." Not that the church was inherently irrelevant, but that Christians were failing to show in concrete ways and to tell in cogent understandable terms how the person of Christ is relevant to all of life in the twentieth century. Elton Trueblood, the influential Quaker teacher and writer, puts it another way. He says, "It is hard to exaggerate the degree to which the modern church seems irrelevant to modern man."

The number one way, then, for Christians to be the salt Christ commands them to be is to teach His relevance, to demonstrate His relevance, to live His relevance in every area of life. We cannot accomplish this by talking only to ourselves, writing only for ourselves, associating only with ourselves and working only in the "safe" careers and professions. Being salt is not nearly so much about having more pastors and missionaries as it is about having many more committed Christian lay people thinking strategically about and acting on ways to build the kingdom in such areas as public policy, advertising, media, higher education, entertainment, the arts, and sports.

Keeping Christ bottled up in the churches is keeping salt in the shakers, and He does not go where we do not take Him. We need to take Him everywhere and show His relevance and the relevance of His Word to every aspect of modern life. This is not an option, it is an imperative, a scriptural imperative.

The process of obeying Christ's command to be salt is about penetration, just as many of Christ's commands are about penetration. Salt must penetrate the meat to preserve it. Christians must penetrate key areas of culture to have a preserving effect. And penetration does not mean standing outside and lobbing hand grenades of criticism over the wall. It is not about being reactionary and negative. It is about being inside through competence and talent and, with God's help and the Holy Spirit's leading, offering scripturally based alternatives to those things that are corrupting and evil.

We need to understand that real Christian penetration is not easy. For example, it is infinitely easier to boycott objectionable television programs than it is to create, produce, sell, and distribute a quality television program or series that would extol virtue, family values, Christian courage, and eternal truths. Participating in a boycott of the products of companies sponsoring trashy television programs might make us feel good and righteous, but it has very little to do with being salt in the world. It certainly does not call for the kind of commitment Christ asks for. Compare sending a few dollars to the boycott headquarters and refraining from buying a certain brand of soap for a few weeks to committing oneself, one's resources, and one's career to providing for the homes of the nation television programming that would glorify Christ. The first is trivial, almost frivolous, the second worthy of prayerful support and sacrificial commitment. When Christians criticize, carp, and complain but offer no alternatives, the world rolls its eyes, snickers, and moves on. It is really only when we offer a "more excellent way" that we command or deserve much attention.

Dr. Ray Pritchard, Bible scholar and the senior pastor of Calvary Memorial Church in Oak Park, Illinois, says, "Being the salt of the earth means acting as a purifying agent to hinder the spread of evil. We who follow Jesus Christ are to be a 'moral disinfectant' stopping the spread of evil. We are to be the conscience of the community, speaking out for what is true and right."

To do that, we must be in that community. We must be a part of that community. We cannot be much of a "moral disinfectant" from afar. It does very little good to commiserate with each other about how evil the "Hollywood community" is, or how godless the television community is, or how the print media seems to always take the low road, or how government policy makers seem to never consider biblical truths, or how corrupt the music and arts scenes are. Sitting in the pews wringing our hands about decay in the world is not being salt. Neither is decrying the evil without offering positive alternatives.

Certainly, there's much in this world that is alarming, but I believe there's a better way to do something about it than simply preach against it. The best way to stop the spread of evil is to replace it with something good.

The best way to stop the spread of popular music with its vulgar suggestive lyrics is to record great music that uplifts the human spirit. Christian artist Amy Grant retards the spread of evil every time one of her records plays on a secular radio station. Those who criticize her for "crossing over" into the secular world with music that is not distinctly Christian forget one thing. Her music takes up the air time that could have gone to one of the multitude of recordings offering only degradation and moral rot. Amy Grant is being salt in the world. She's high on my list of candidates for a Roaring Lamb Hall of Fame. One Amy Grant hit record provides more salt for a decaying world than a thousand sermons decrying the evils of popular music or nationwide boycotts of recording companies. We need more Amy Grants much more than we need more reactionary sermons. We also need Christian musicians, talent managers, producers, and record-company executives to bring real salt to the whole influential popular music industry.

Don't get me wrong. There are times when following the call of God demands that we speak out loudly against flagrant evil. But if that's all we do, particularly if most of our speaking out is only to each other, we are not being salt. The way to be salt is to replace evil with good, not to just sound off against the evil.

The Genesis account of Sodom and Gomorrah is very instructive about the preserving power of righteous people and illustrates the way God's people bring the saving salt to every situation. As long as there were even a few righteous people within Sodom, God spared it. Even when Lot was the only righteous person within the city, it was preserved until he left. Today, Christians are called to occupy the lost provinces of society and hold on to "the last man" the way Lot did. We need to abandon the mentality that some professions are just too corrupt for Christians to enter. We are called to be the Lots of every legitimate area of human endeavor, preserving it from the wrath of God. The longer we preserve it and the longer we act as salt there, the more opportunity there will be for men and women to be won to the person of Christ. Being salt does not always mean we "evangelize," but by replacing evil with good, we enhance the climate for evangelism.

In the life of the Spirit, in the battle of good vs. evil, in the effort to preserve goodness, there are no effective salt substitutes. If Christians do not provide the salt, it's not there, and life loses much of its flavor, much of its meaningfulness. Consider the history of Christianity in Europe. Over the past twenty or so years, I have made more than a hundred visits to London. One year I spent more time in London than in any other city except my home city of Dallas. Using our apartment in Paris as a base, I have become very familiar with the great capital cities of Europe. Sadly, these cities and their societies are increasingly secular and humanistic to the point that they are almost pagan. The church may be physically present, but much of its spiritual vitality has been sapped and is, for all practical purposes, gone. And as dynamic, relevant Christianity has gone, so too has the life-enhancing taste of salt that Christians bring to life and living. Even in these glamorous tourist destinations, which everyone wants to visit, once you get past the intrigue and into the lives of the people you do not need to be particularly perceptive to notice the existential *angst* that seems to have everyone in its grip. There's no salt. Conspicuously absent is the sharpness and spice brought to a society by the penetrating salt of an active church.

Will the same thing happen here? Some say it's already happening. Because of our historic ties with Europe and Great

Britain, these areas are, perhaps, the most revealing examples of what a society once mightily influenced by the message of Christ can become when it becomes almost totally secularized and the church survives primarily as an anachronism. Certainly there are dynamic Christians and wonderful churches in both Britain and Europe, but the numbers are now so small as to be demographically insignificant. To use Alfred North Whitehead's phrase about the church, "Its institutions no longer direct the patterns of life." It is irrelevant. There is no salt.

In America, with all our problems—the extreme secularization of society with its accompanying commitment to instant gratification—the church still provides a measure of salt for our society. Not enough, but it is still there, adding flavor to our lives. The trend, however, is toward the secular, the profane, the here and now. If we are content to let that continue, all we need to do is stay the course and keep preaching to each other as we watch a culture fade into oblivion. But if we want to see our society revitalized, we need to add some salt. We need to let the lambs roar.

I've spent a good deal of my professional career in two arenas: professional sports and television. I may be biased, but I don't think you could name two more influential fields. From highly visible athletes to a steady stream of programming into your homes, these two fields are truly culture shaping. And they illustrate both the best and the worst of Christian involvement in the world.

Certainly, anyone following big-time sports in America is well aware of its problems. Dishonesty, exploitation, drugs, illicit sex, ego gratification gone out of control, and the attempt to deify money are all very significant problems not only for professional sports but also for college sports and, in some communities, even high school sports. In his best-seller, *Friday Night Lights*, H. G. Bissinger gives us a chilling picture of how high school football in

Odessa, Texas, mirrors many of the worst problems of professional sports. However, with all its problems, there is a Christian presence within organized sports that makes life in that community more interesting, dynamic, and meaningful than in many professional communities. This is because Christians made a deliberate, strategic decision years ago to actively and effectively infiltrate that community with the salt of the Gospel.

More than in any other area of American life, Christians are providing salt in almost every activity involving sports. The Fellowship of Christian Athletes provides a ministry for almost every high school and college in America. Athletes In Action provides a way for Christian athletes to use their athletic skills to win a hearing for the Gospel message. Every team in Major League Baseball, the National Football League, and the National Basketball Association has a chaplain, who provides for everything from weekly chapel services to in-depth discipling of team members and coaches. To cite just one example, Dave Dravecky, the courageous former major league pitcher who lost his arm to cancer, credits the discipling efforts of the baseball chaplains in San Diego and San Francisco with helping him to move toward maturity in Christ through systematic study of God's Word.

There is a Christian ministry devoted exclusively to the professional golf tour and one devoted exclusively to the professional tennis tour. Even the pro bass-fishing tour has chapel services.

There is almost no athletic gathering of any kind without a significant Christian component. The World Series, the Super Bowl, the Olympics, All-Star Games in all pro sports, major coaching conventions, and NCAA meetings all have prayer breakfasts, luncheons with Christian speakers, or special Bible studies. In addition, there is almost always a companion activity for or outreach to the wives.

Former Detroit sports writer Waddy Spoelstra edits an influential monthly publication called *Closer Walk* with the subtitle *The Christian Sports Insider*. The December 1991 edition carried this banner headline across the entire front page of the paper: "Superstar David Robinson Accepts Jesus Christ." The story describes how the seven-foot San Antonio Spurs center was led to Christ by the Spurs' chaplain. This paper is representative of sports' unself-conscious approach to the Gospel.

Most important, many well-known stars as well as movers and shakers in sports make their commitment to Christ very public. Such Hall of Fame caliber names as Tom Landry and Roger Staubach in football, Julius Irving in basketball, Orel Hershiser and radio announcer Ernie Harwell in baseball, and Stan Smith in tennis are only a representative few who openly and avidly proclaim Christ.

I do not mean to imply that the world of big-time sports is one great big Sunday school picnic. You and I both know it isn't. But it is an arena in which the Christian message is welcome, where individuals are not scorned because they believe in Jesus, and where some of the most highly respected leaders are known as much for their Christian commitment as for their athletic or managerial skill. Can you say that about the arena in which you work?

The reason why Christian faith is present in the sports community is that Christians did not run away the minute alcohol was served in a stadium, when games were played on Sunday, when gambling entered the picture. Instead, they reasoned that because some of these troubling elements were a part of sports, that was all the more reason for Christians to stay and add as much salt as possible.

And yet one of the first criticisms I overheard when I decided to go with the Miami Dolphins was "How can he be a Christian and work for an organization that promotes sports on Sunday?"

The contrast between sports and television can hardly be greater. In sports you meet Christians everywhere you go. In more than twenty years of working in television, I have met almost no openly confessing Christian working in mainstream television. The difference in the two communities can hardly be more pronounced. In sports, active Christians provide a life-enhancing seasoning just not present in television. Is it any wonder, then, that most of what is available on our home screens is so lacking in Judeo-Christian content? How can these television people be expected to accurately portray Christian values on the screen if there aren't any Christian producers, screenwriters, cameramen, or directors?

I went into the world of sports with very little encouragement from the church. I would venture to say there is even less encouragement within the church for someone to take his résumé to Burbank and interview for a job with NBC. And we expect television to promote our values?

I will look at television in greater detail in later chapters, but let me take this opportunity to address some of the criticisms leveled at those who uphold the Christian presence in athletics. It goes something like this: with all the dynamic Christians involved, all the sports-related Christian ministries, and all the Christian influence at almost every level of sports, evil still exists and even grows. That's absolutely right, but as my friend Dr. Pritchard points out, "Salt retards spoilage. It doesn't prevent the process of decay, but it slows it down...." I shudder to think about the condition of sports without Christian influence. Certainly there is still much that is wrong with sports, but I believe things would be worse if Christians had fled this arena. Our job as Christians is not to take over the various communities in our world; it is, however, to penetrate them, to be present, to provide God's alternatives to evil, to demonstrate Christ's relevance there, to be as good a representative as possible for Him and His church.

Too many Christians are more concerned about keeping score than being salt. The problem with this mindset is that we will not "win" in the way the world sees winning. Even if the church and its people do a very effective job of penetrating a particular community, as is the case with sports, evil will not be eliminated until our Lord returns and establishes His new kingdom. Salt retards spoilage, it doesn't prevent it. It slows down decay, it doesn't stop it. Our responsibility is not to keep score but to keep living for Him. We know the ultimate victory will be ours through Christ. It will not, however, happen here. If we are effective, we will have many triumphs, many victories, many thrills as we see the Holy Spirit turn our efforts into positive benefits in the lives of some of those around us, but evil will survive, even prosper. We are called to be our best and to leave the results to Him.

The scorekeeping mentality is most pervasive in the way Christians approach television. The well-meaning Christian people working so ineffectively to improve television in America spend much of their time monitoring telecasts so they can tell us how many acts of violence, how many sexually explicit scenes, how many anti-Christian plots are seen on the nation's networks. Again, it seems to me, that our job is not so much to monitor evil as it is to provide alternatives to evil. If the resources used to survey all those hours of television, report those results, and then organize a boycott had been used to produce and distribute even one quality national program that pointed viewers to the more excellent way, that would be of more value than all the scorekeeping. And it would be much closer to fulfilling Christ's command to be salt in the world.

Sports teaches us another lesson about being salt, and it applies to all other fields of endeavor. We do not have to be the best to be effective, but we do have to be at our best.

Byron Ballard never progressed beyond the minor leagues as a baseball pitcher, but, because he was a solid, hard-working teammate, he won a hearing for the Gospel with Dave Dravecky while they were playing at Amarillo, Texas. Dave accepted Christ and went on to become an outstanding major league pitcher who was a powerful influence for good in the highest levels of baseball and continues to minister to many. Byron went for it. He used his skills and abilities to penetrate the professional baseball community, performed at his own personal peak, and after he had earned a hearing, effectively presented the Gospel message. Byron did not make it to the major leagues, but his influence did. Byron Ballard is the salt of the earth.

That's the kind of salt most of you reading this book can be. That's the kind of roaring lamb I'd like to see moving into every culture-shaping venue of our land.

Christians of both competence and commitment are needed to penetrate every area of society, and they need to do it with Christ's command to be salt firmly in mind. When the church sees only the professional ministry as a calling of concern, as a field of interest for the whole body, as a profession to be supported with prayer and financial support, kingdom building is terribly weakened.

How many churches have a strategy that seeks in very concrete measurable ways to equip its people to be salt every day and consciously targets areas of its community for penetration? Not nearly enough. This is much more difficult and requires much more thought than spending our time and effort promoting Sunday church attendance, special evangelism seminars, and a yearly missionary conference. Being a roaring lamb is not about special days, special emphases, special people, and special professions. Rather, it is about everyday people doing everyday jobs with a very special goal—that of effectively representing Christ in all areas of society. Our churches should exist for this.

At the very least, the young people of the church should be made to see that their careers, whatever they may be, are just as vital, just as much a concern of the congregation, and just as much a part of the mission of the church as are those of the foreign missionaries the church supports. This is in no way a call to support missionaries less, but does it seem right to have a budget for, sermon series about, and special emphasis on missionaries and to ignore the young people of the local congregation who will be heading into areas of life just as difficult and just as demanding as far as living out Christ's command to be salt and light is concerned as those entered into by any missionary?

Typically, the young people of a congregation who are called to the professional ministry are singled out for special attention, special counseling, special prayer, and special financial support. Why shouldn't talented young people of the congregation who hope to enter medicine or teaching, or journalism, or writing, or plumbing, or retailing, or any other world of work be given at least the same kind of attention? At the very least, they should be made to understand that in their careers they have both the possibility and the responsibility to be a part of the ministry of the church. At the very least they should be instructed in the how of this as well as the why. Also at the very least they should know that they are valued, being prayed for, and supported as they take the salt of the Gospel to their place of work every day. This is the way to make sure they become roaring lambs.

It is clear that the Scripture commands us to be salt in the world. It is clear that this demands penetration—not selective penetration but penetration of every area of society. It is clear that the command is to every Christian—not to some elite, professional class of Christians. It is clear that the way to be salt is to provide positive uplifting alternatives wherever we are as opposed to being negative and reactionary. It is clear that the call to be salt calls for both competence and commitment—we must be at our best in order to win the kind of hearing Christ deserves. It is clear that churches must consistently, consciously, and conscientiously provide an equipping ministry for the entire congregation, particularly for its young people if Christ's command is to be carried out. It is clear that life anywhere without salt is bland and tasteless and is decaying at a faster rate than it should. It is clear that there is a price to be paid for being salt. The world will not always appreciate being stung by the salt of God's Word. It is clear that the command to be salt requires very little scorekeeping. Our responsibility is to do our best and to leave the results with Him in the knowledge that the ultimate victory is ours through Christ.

Finally, it is clear that the culture-shaping professions are especially salt-free. So the remainder of this book will take a closer look at some of those professions and challenge you to consider how you can be part of a mighty effort to reclaim those territories that we have given up.

The only way we can do that is to find some lambs who are willing to roar.

> "Whoever acknowledges me before men, I will also acknowledge him before my Father in heaven."
>
> Matthew 10:32

3

Where Are All the Christians?

Who speaks for Christians in America today? Who, on a regular basis, effectively brings a biblical Christian perspective to bear on the great issues of our society in ways that force consideration by both the masses and the movers and shakers? Where are the Christian op-ed pieces (a page of special features usually opposite the editorial page of a newspaper) in the *New York Times*? Who is the regular guest on *Crossfire* who stands up for a Christian world view? Who is writing the well-reasoned "white papers" that show the soundness of a biblical approach to homelessness, AIDS, child abuse, poverty, crime, drugs, and the dysfunctional family? When the editors of *USA Today* want a quote from a recognized Christian spokesperson, whom do they call? Have you seen any Christian apologists lately on *Larry King Live*?

Okay, maybe moving into the national arena is a bit of a stretch. So who in your local community speaks publicly and forcefully—yet with grace and compassion—for a Christian point of view? Who presents the Christian perspective soundly and with good humor on local talk shows? Who is writing the quality guest editorials and letters to the editor in your local newspaper that challenge readers with biblical answers to current questions? Who is supplying the salt of the Gospel in your town?

What strategy is your own church pursuing to provide the salt in areas of local public policy? Does your strategy consist solely of your pastor's preaching against the "pervasive evils of our day"? What is the strategy and what are the tactics your church is using to retard the growth of evil in your city, town, or village? What positive alternatives are people in your congregation making available to people in your community? What are your methods of "speaking" to people outside the four walls of your church? How is your church working to demonstrate the relevance of Christ to taxes, housing, mass transit, and education in your city?

When the average person in your town thinks of a Christian, who comes to his mind? Jim Bakker? Jimmy Swaggart? Robert Tilton? Is there a single layperson in your community who is known as an articulate advocate for a Christian point of view?

How does your church respond to media distortions, misconception, and misinformation about Christians and their motives? Do you have a response? I like the *Life Application Bible*'s commentary on Ephesians 5:10–14. It says, "God needs people who will take a stand for what is right. Christians must lovingly speak out for what is true and right." The admonition here is for a positive loving response to evil, distortions, and error. We are to speak out for what is true and right. Again, to speak out for what is true and right requires more than just railing against evil. The call is for rational, cogent, well-crafted presentations of positive alternatives gleaned from the Scriptures. Is your church encouraging and helping its members to be part of this kind of ministry? Are you honing and then using your own talents and abilities in this kind of ministry? Or is your only response to evil in your community a boycott or gripe session with a few other members of your Bible-study group?

In short, are you or your church in the mainstream of dialogue in your community with regard to decisions that affect the quality of life there?

In the wolfpack of political and social discourse, are you a roaring lamb?

We can be thankful that there are a few Christians with significant talent who have combined competence and commitment to attain positions as syndicated newspaper columnists. William Murchison, whose column is distributed by Creators Syndicate, writes with erudition and power and often takes the church to task for its failures and shortcomings in the battle of good versus evil. He does this as a committed layman in the Episcopal Church. The enormously talented Cal Thomas is an even more regular and more forceful advocate for a biblical perspective in his columns distributed by the *Los Angeles Times* syndicate. He often quotes Scripture. Remember, he's not writing for a Christian magazine or newspaper but for the *LA Times* as well as a number of other papers that pick up his column. In a recent column on Magic Johnson and AIDS he wrote, "How wonderful it would have been had Magic Johnson stood before the press and the watching world and said, 'Avoid sexual looseness like the plague. Every other sin that a man commits is done outside his own body, but this is an offense against his own body.' That's from the Bible. America's most banned book. Ask yourself why condoms are now distributed in public schools, but the Bible and the principles it contains are banned and you have a clue as to why our cultural fabric is unraveling. Its truths, however, ring with new clarity in the age of AIDS." In the same column he goes on to quote Senate chaplain Richard Halverson and then to extol the efficacy of prayer.

The columns of both Murchison and Thomas have the enormous advantage of appearing, not in the religion section of newspapers but in the editorial pages right alongside the columns of William F. Buckley, Jack Anderson, Russell Baker, Evans and Novak, Mike Royko, and George Will. Does your church care how many times the Murchison and Thomas columns run in your local paper if at all? Do you and your fellow church members let the publisher of your local paper know how much you appreciate these columnists and how you wish they would run more regularly? Is there any strategy to see that these columnists have a voice in the newspapers that serve your community?

Let me make one thing perfectly clear. I'm not calling for yet another official statement from the National Association of Evangelicals or some other Christian organization. Nor am I calling for one of the many fine Christian leaders to step up to the national podium and issue "official" Christian positions on the many issues facing us. Even if it would be possible to get Christians to coalesce behind one person, which it is not, this approach is limiting and ultimately self-defeating. We've tried it before and it just doesn't work.

Instead, I'm calling for individual Christians to become roaring lambs—informed citizens who will enter their community dialogues on social and political issues. I'm also calling for local congregations to develop strategies for making sure they are always a part of their community's policy-setting process. In his small but monumentally important book *The Company of the Committed*, Elton Trueblood wrote, "The test of the vitality of a religion is to be seen in its effect on culture." If a religion is really vital, meaningful, relevant, and important, it will make a difference not only

in the lives of individuals but also in society itself. Evangelical
Christians in America must face up to this challenge. Our churches
must help us do a better job of being salt—of being roaring lambs.

I live in Dallas, Texas, a community blessed by some of the
biggest and most prestigious churches and evangelical institutions
in America. Powerfully influenced by Dallas Theological Seminary,
a major Christian publisher, several Christian television ministries,
and dozens of great, historically significant churches, it is one of
those three or four Christian "meccas" in this nation. When
Campus Crusade for Christ scheduled their giant "Expo" gathering
in 1985, Dallas was almost automatically selected as its site. When
Sandi Patti and Bill Gaither brought their "Young Messiah" presentation to town, nearly twenty thousand people paid up to seven-
teen dollars a ticket to crowd into the giant Reunion Arena to be
blessed by great Christian music. New megachurches staffed by
well-trained professionals thrive here; they offer biblically sound
doctrine and programs for every age group. Some of the top religious radio stations in the nation are available to listeners here
twenty-four hours a day. It is possible to sit under great Bible teaching and expository preaching every Sunday in the church of your
choice. This is truly a blessed community.

There is, however, a darker, more disturbing picture of Dallas.
In recent years Dallas has been both the "divorce capital" and the
"murder capital" of the nation. A recent magazine article tells us
our city leads the nation in topless bars. Violent crime is a nightly
occurrence in many of the city's neighborhoods. AIDS, drugs, and
prostitution are rampant. Abortion is big business. Race relations
among the black, white, and Hispanic communities are at least as
bad as in any other major American city. Some of the biggest and
most flagrant of the savings-and-loan rip-offs were perpetuated in
the Dallas area.

How do we reconcile these two pictures of Dallas? How can there be such a strong and vital church community while the rest of the city declines morally? The answer is obvious. Dallas has a lot of lambs, but they aren't roaring. They're in their comfortable pews talking to each other instead of venturing out into a dangerous and threatening world. As the debates on many basic issues of life in the city take place, they are, for the most part, conducted without the light of a Christian perspective being cast on the subject.

Consider the example of Dallas Theological Seminary, which sits almost in the shadows of the glass-and-steel towers of downtown Dallas. Among its faculty are many gifted Bible scholars and teachers. Many are noted writers with several books in print. Graduates of the seminary fill many area pulpits and staff many Christian organizations here. Yet the seminary has almost no discernible voice in the city. No one from the seminary regularly writes for the local newspaper or comments publicly on the life going on in the city around it. It does a great job of educating a professional class of Christians. It certainly influences the churches here for good, but it is almost as if the city that surrounds it doesn't exist except in its churches. Salt is present in great amounts; its application is questionable.

Dallas and its seminary are not unique. They are, rather, all too representative of American cities, their churches, and Christian institutions. The church is hardly involved in the life going on around it. Neither do individual Christians seem to be empowered to provide the salt so desperately needed. They make no impact on the culture. Our Christianity fails Trueblood's test of vitality. Evangelical Christian thought, ideas, and ideals are not shaping today's American society. Of even more concern is the reality that they are not a part of the important discussions and debates. They are not put forward regularly and effectively in any of the forums that count. We talk to and write for each other, sometimes brilliantly, but with little impact on the world around us. What we need are Christian speakers and writers to address the vast non-Christian audience on topics of vital concern to them.

This chapter opened by asking who speaks for Christians in America today. The truest answer unfortunately is that there is no one. Remember, I'm not calling for some "official" spokesperson. We've got quite a few of those. Nor am I calling for more articles in Christian books and magazines. What we need is a whole group of gifted Christian writers and speakers to begin to win a hearing for biblical truths in publications and on broadcasts that reach the mainstream of Americans.

And believe me, it's possible. This is not a pipe dream. Take, for instance, the field of print media. Good, solid, creative writing will find its way onto the pages of your local newspaper, the *New York Times*, or *Newsweek* if the writer expands his or her vision to include the markets served by these publications. But too often, a well-meaning pastor sends a copy of his best sermon to the local newspaper editor and then preaches out in that sermon about the paper's intolerance to Christian thought and values. Frankly, most sermons don't belong in a secular newspaper or magazine, and we do our cause a disservice when we submit this type of writing for publication.

The way to win a hearing—to be given print space and air time—is to be articulate, cogent, and good-natured. Quoting lots of Scripture and using the evangelical jargon that only one's fellow church members understand is viewed by secular editors as inappropriate, and I agree. Such writing is the bleating of lambs. We want those lambs to roar, don't we?

Of course, not all Christians are gifted with the ability to write a compelling op-ed piece for their daily newspaper, but many are.

Not every Christian has the verbal skills, public recognition, and camera presence to make a successful appearance on *Larry King Live*, but some do. But do we encourage such involvement? Has your pastor urged you to develop this skill to the glory of God?

Since important forums exist both locally and nationally, many pens, many voices are needed. In the field of print and electronic journalism, many Christians can become effective advocates. Many churches can be more relevant by regularly and systematically equipping and empowering their members for this kind of ministry.

Consider just one example of this kind of ministry. The *Wall Street Journal*, concerned as it is with "money and markets," is one of the most secular of publications. It is also one of the most influential. Its national circulation is exceeded only by that of *USA Today*. Because of its powerful and significant readership, its impact is much more important. Recently the following appeared in the letters-to-the-editor column:

EVANGELICAL MISSIONS: HERE'S THE GOOD NEWS

I was disappointed as I read your October 16 International Page article "Evangelicals, Stressing Cures for Masses' Misery, Make Inroads in Roman Catholic Latin America," because you collectively lump all evangelical churches into a distinction that only the most extreme cults share, that of an "emphasis . . . on demonology, exorcism and miraculous cures. . . ."

The word "evangelical" is derived from a Greek word meaning good news or good message. The good news or message is that Jesus Christ died on the cross to save all those who respond to Him for their sin and its result—eternal separation from God. The evangelical movement preaches that this gift is available through God's grace by faith in Christ for His work on the cross. Thus, the focus of the legitimate evangelical church is on Jesus Christ and the salvation He offers through His work, not on demonology and miraculous healing.

You intimate that the Catholic Church's sole focus is on saving souls. You contrast that with what you call the Protestant evangelical movements' focus on "pragmatism" and "mysticism." What you don't say is that for every extremist sect practicing mysticism, there are many more legitimate evangelical Christian missions operating in Brazil and all over South America, concerned with saving souls for Christ, and, conversely, many Roman Catholic bishops who practice politics.

Wow! That's what I call a roaring lamb. Presumably the writer is a layman, for he signed his name without any title or without noting any association. Just an individual from a small town in Illinois who saw a way to enter the national discourse in a way that will do some good. And what a job he did! In three brief, well-written paragraphs, he corrected error, promoted Christian missions, and gave a beautifully clear account of the gospel message. And he did it in the *Wall Street Journal!* But why should this happen so infrequently?

Now, maybe the writer of the WSJ letter is a genius and just sat down and knocked out this little gem in ten minutes or so. I doubt it. I like to picture him sitting at his desk prayerfully considering every word, trying one construction and then another, crossing out and rewriting, polishing the piece perhaps until it was, well, not perfect but crafted to be just as good as he could possibly make it. I like to see him as "a workman who does not need to be ashamed and who correctly handles the word of truth" (2 Tim. 2:15).

Among the most important accomplishments of the *Wall Street Journal* letter is that it corrected error. Error and misconception about what Christians really believe and what the Bible really teaches are rampant. It is tragic when the great saving good that Christ can bring to an individual and that Christianity can bring to a society are rejected when the truths of both are understood. It is an unmitigated disaster when rejection is based on misinformation and factual error. But the unfortunate reason that error lives so long, feeds on itself, and grows so abundantly is that Christians are the most underrepresented group in the arena of public-policy discussion and debate in America today. We are just not in the ball game. Because we have abandoned the high ground, Christian thought—when it is considered at all—is considered quaintly irrelevant at best and mean and bigoted at worst.

On the other hand, the specific agendas of our nation's minority and special-interest groups are advanced far more energetically than those of Christians. Far-out animal-rights extremists get more consideration than do Christian thinkers. Why? Because they are at least out there. They have thought carefully and strategically about how they are going to influence the public. They are in the fray. We aren't, which helps explain why Christian ideas and values are so easily dismissed, even ridiculed. No one in public life wants to offend blacks, Jews, gays, or women. But hardly anyone worries too much about offending Christians. Art, literature, movies, music, and television can be anti-Christian with impunity. Politicians regularly put forth anti-Christian positions. No one ever calls them into account in a measured, intellectually persuasive, gently instructive way. Rather than meet such animosity in the arena of public discourse, our usual approach is to complain about it in sermons, Christian radio and television programs, or Christian publications. When we do that, we're preaching to the choir. We make ourselves feel good, but we haven't done a thing to change the situation. The place to correct an error in the *New York Times* is in the *New York Times*. And, again, just pointing out the fact of the error is only half the job. Laying out the truth in clear, understandable terms is equally important, as is articulating viable Christian alternatives.

Take, for example, the way in which the pro-abortion movement has entered the mainstream and gained respectability. Pro-abortionists score very well for their cause when they forcefully, and too often correctly, point out that the zeal of prolifers seems to wane when confronted with the real needs of children who are allowed to be born. With biting and telling sarcasm, they ask where the marchers and demonstrators are when children go to school hungry, live in squalor and disease, are hijacked into the pornography trade, and are abused in ever-growing numbers. It is always easier to protest, to carry a placard than it is to do the hard work of providing the cup of cold water in His name. (Besides, the cup of cold water rarely attracts television coverage.) The pro-life movement will never succeed to the extent it should until its advocates and all Christians work just as hard to produce good as we do to denounce evil. We always need to present positive Christian alternatives.

The primary reason that there is so much error and so few Christian alternatives being considered in the ongoing flow of public policy discourse, is that basically evangelical Christians have abdicated. We have left the field. It is almost as if we are afraid to venture out into the world of ideas—to have our beliefs go head to head with those of other beliefs. We say we believe that God's Word relates to all of life and has the answers to all of life's questions. Yet we primarily spend our time and energies talking only to each other, writing only for each other, performing only for each other. This abdication has made it possible, even necessary, for evangelical Christians and their beliefs to be interpreted to the world primarily by non-Christians. The fact that they almost always get it wrong is our fault, not theirs.

This abdication has produced mass ignorance and misinformation. Alan Dershowitz, a brilliant Jewish legal scholar and advocate, displays an amazing ignorance of Christian motivations and attitudes in his recent best seller, *Chutzpah*. Our fault not his. Even Christian vocabulary has been distorted and debased. Words and phrases that should have a very good connotation—fundamentalist, commitment, evangelism, born again, Bible-based—are misunderstood, and given a negative slant. Evangelical Christians of talent and intellect are not out there in public life correcting misunderstanding, gently teaching what Christians really believe, effectively showing how Christians really live.

As one who has worked most of his life in professional sports, I admire competent professionalism. I usually disdain the amateur, dabbler, and dilettante. Give me the old pro every time. However, my call here is for Christians who have maintained their amateur standing. It is my firm belief that the most effective spokespersons for Jesus Christ in the public arena will:

1. Have never asked for money on radio or television.
2. Not be on the payroll of any Christian organization.
3. Through competence and class in their own "secular" profession, have earned the right to be heard.
4. Be an excellent communicator.
5. Know and love God's Word.
6. Understand that Christianity is relevant to all of life.

I can almost hear the groans of disbelief. The conventional wisdom will say that our best spokespersons are the Chuck Swindolls and the James Dobsons of the church. Their great followings will be cited, as will their communications skills and their commitment to the truth of Scripture. But for the lambs to start roaring, we need to set aside this conventional wisdom and quit hoping that these marvelous Christian teachers will carry the ball for us.

Now don't get me wrong. Although I have never met Chuck Swindoll or heard him preach in person, no one has spoken to me more clearly and persuasively over the past few years. I am an avid listener to his radio program, his taped sermons are in my car tape deck all the time, and his books are in my home. His Bible teaching has blessed my life in many ways. I am thankful for Chuck Swindoll, for his ministry to me and my family. As I travel in Christian circles, I hear only words of appreciation for Rev. Swindoll and his ministry.

But, guess what. Out where I spend my professional life—in the headquarters of the television networks along the Avenue of the Americas in New York, in the advertising agencies a few blocks away on Madison Avenue, and in the offices of the professional sports leagues—people have never heard of Chuck Swindoll.

It is almost exactly the same with James Dobson. The Christian family in America is being served extraordinarily well by the Dobson ministry. My own grandchildren are being raised according to Dobson principles. I am thankful for this. Recently, a friend of mine, Dave Dravecky, was a featured guest on Dr. Dobson's radio program. He was amazed at the volume of the response he received. And everywhere I went in the week following Dave's appearance on the program, Christians were discussing these shows. It seemed that everyone had tuned in. However, out there in the world at large, the program had no discernible impact. But when Dave was on the ABC program *20/20* with Barbara Walters, the rest of the world took notice. Whether you like her program or not, that show has real impact. All my friends in the industry knew about Dave Dravecky after that one interview on *20/20*. Incidentally, when people in my world mentioned the *20/20* appearance, I made it a point to ask if they had also caught Dave with James Dobson. The almost universal response was, "With whom?"

Please, please don't think I am demeaning Chuck Swindoll or James Dobson in any way. They both have extraordinarily effective ministries. Even though I do not know either one personally, I am deeply thankful for what they do for me and my family. It is important, however, to understand the scope of their ministries and those of other Christian professionals, because if we don't, we will never make a real impact on our world.

Chuck Swindoll and James Dobson speak to Christians. They are heard, for the most part, on Christian radio stations, their books are carried, for the most part, in Christian bookstores. They are equippers. Their job is to instruct and inspire Christians so we will go out and do our jobs, so we will go out and be salt. They and many other dedicated professionals do their job extraordinarily well. It's we, the lambs, who are lying down on the job. We are not applying what they are teaching us.

I must add that it is irresponsible and unscriptural for us to expect Swindoll, Dobson, et al. to do our jobs for us. The call, the command to be salt, is a universal one to all Christian men and women. We can't hire anyone, even Chuck Swindoll or James Dobson, to do this job for us. There are no substitutes in this game. The professionals are the coaches, and we laymen have to be the players. Their responsibility is to be sure we are equipped, that our best players get in the game at the right positions, and that there is a solid game plan.

How will this happen? How can we make sure a clear, winsome Christian voice is heard in America today? Christian writers, scholars, speakers—communicators of all kinds should be involved at the highest level of their abilities. It may be that the Christian school teacher in a small town may be the perfect "designated hitter" to contribute articles for or to write letters to the editor of the weekly newspaper in town. Others may have the ability to draft guest editorials or op-ed pieces for the larger metropolitan daily newspaper. A very few others who have risen to the top of their careers may be alert for the opportunity to speak in a thoughtful measured way about a biblical truth on *Face the Nation* or *Meet the Press*. Everyone should perform up to his or her ability.

Recently, I saw a graduate of a small Christian college I attended testifying on television before a congressional committee. He was fabulous—poised, articulate, persuasive. Because he has been blessed with a superior intellect, good looks, and a pleasing personality and has worked very hard, he has risen to the highest levels of his profession. He not only is called to testify before Congress, he also commands newspaper space and television time almost whenever he wants them. He has won a hearing for what he has to say through diligence, competence, and talent.

Away from the spotlight, he works quietly in Christian causes. It is obvious that he is still committed to Christ and His kingdom. My question is, Why can't he use the "bully pulpit" that his God-given talent has provided for him to unself-consciously be a spokesperson for Christ, showing His relevance to all of life? His stature would give him access to major publications and broadcast opportunities. He has chosen, as far as I know, not to use any public platforms to speak for Christ. I think this is a mistake.

We should be thankful for every Christian in Congress and the administration. There are some wonderful men and women in these positions. Their Christianity is, however, all very private. It is thought to be unseemly and, more particularly, impolitic for them to actively and publicly display their faith. For many years, the strategy for Christians in government has been to meet quietly, almost furtively, for prayer, Bible study, and fellowship. There are obviously some compelling reasons for them to do this. I wonder, however, how this squares with Christ's command to be salt and with His words in Matthew 10:32: "'Whoever acknowledges me before men, I will also acknowledge him before my Father in heaven.'"

I wonder what would happen if a senator, congressman, or cabinet member appearing on *This Week With David Brinkley* would say on camera, "David, we are going to be discussing some very vital and sensitive issues on your show today. Before we begin, I wonder if we could have just a brief word of prayer." What would happen? Would the network pull the plug on the show? Would the guys with big nets and in white coats be waiting to haul him off to a rubber room? Would the president demand his resignation from the cabinet or his constituents immediately mount a recall campaign? What would happen? What would you think if you were watching the U.S. House of Representatives on C-Span and when your own congressman got up to address the house, he openly based his remarks on scriptural truth, intelligently delineated how this persuaded him to vote a certain way, and urged his fellow representatives to vote the same way? What would you think? Would you say, "Whoa! I believe in the Bible and all that, but this is going too far"? Is God's Word truly relevant or not? Are we to be salt or not? Will the lambs never roar?

I freely admit that what I'm suggesting sounds so farfetched as to seem almost ridiculous. But why is that? Why does it seem so stupid to openly be who we are? Why should it be fashionable to keep the most important aspect of our lives in a closet? Gays don't. Radical feminists don't. A modern, "politically correct" position we often hear is "A person's religion is personal and private between him and God. It is no one else's business and shouldn't be publicly displayed." Is this scriptural? Can we be all Christ expects us to be in a closet? Can we be the salt He commands us to be when we refuse to acknowledge His "ownership" of our lives? Certainly, we need to be sensitive and respectful. We need to choose our battles wisely, and we must earn the right to be heard. But we are still commanded to be salt, and it seems to me that includes being salt in the spotlight of public life.

Now here is a powerful example of just how possible it is to be a roaring lamb. Johnny Hart burst onto the scene as a major cartoonist with the creation of "The Wizard of Id" and the "B.C." cartoon strips. Those two strips, distributed by Creators Syndicate, are among the most widely carried by the nation's newspapers. Fans of the two strips and of Mr. Hart enjoy both the sharp-edged humor and the evocative drawing. But Mr. Hart startled many with what has now become known as "The Good Friday Strip" by using his well-earned position in the nation's newspapers to make a powerful statement about the meaning of Easter:

Some papers, notably the *Los Angeles Times*, refused to run this strip. Thankfully, most, including my local paper, did. As I read the comic section on Good Friday morning (hey, I *like* the funnies!), I was stunned when I came to "B.C." I read and re-read it to make sure I wasn't seeing things. I'm sure millions of people around the country did too, Christians as well as non-Christians. Johnny Hart "roared" in a provocative and telling way. In fact, I was so excited about this loud and beautiful roar that I wrote the cartoonist and now have a signed copy of the original cartoon hanging on the wall right next to my own Emmy. And Mr. Hart goes into my personal Roaring Lambs Hall of Fame. Who says it's farfetched to think we can take our faith with us into the real world?

If the lambs will ever roar—if Christian faith is ever to gain acceptance in our culture—churches and Christian colleges must do a better job of addressing the paucity of a Christian presence in American public life. The best way to start is to admit there's a problem. Set aside all those glowing church-growth statistics and acknowledge that Christian thought and values are almost completely absent in the mainstream of American culture. The only thing keeping us from such an admission is pride, and we all know what follows pride. So just admit it. We're not where we should be as people of God.

Second, we must be convinced that with God's help we can make a difference. You see, on the one hand we have this inflated opinion of how we're changing the world, and almost in the same breath we say, "Well, God never promised we would 'Christianize' the world." Of course He didn't, but that doesn't excuse us from letting our salt serve as a preserving agent in culture. We can correct error at its source. We can show the relevance of Christ to every aspect of modern life. We can put forward a Christian worldview. We can show how biblical values make sense. We can be honest and open about who we are and what we believe, making it more difficult for the so-called "minority" views of secularists to shape our world.

Third, we must be deliberate. Every church and every Christian organization should develop its own strategy for positively engaging culture in its neighborhood, community, and state. The strategy must depend on lay people for its execution. Every local church needs to encourage and develop writers and speakers for every level of involvement. Let me also add that the church at large needs to encourage the very able Christian writers and speakers we already have to share their talent with the secular press. In many ways, *Christianity Today* and the *Christian Century* are the practice court. The game is being played in the *New York Times, USA Today, Newsweek*, and *TIME*. It is not being played in your local church newsletter; it is being played in local daily newspapers. The game is not in the Christian bookstores but in B Dalton and Waldenbooks. Even though Christian books often outsell those listed on the *New York Times* Best Seller List, it's the *New York Times* list that counts. This game is not being played on the *700 Club*, on the *Hour of Power*, or on Christian radio stations. That's only practice. The game is on *Meet the Press, Face the Nation*, and on your local mainstream radio and television stations.

Do we have a strategy for getting our best and brightest writers and thinkers into these arenas, or are we satisfied to keep them to ourselves?

I began this chapter by asking who speaks for Christians today? The answer is simple. You do. Not your pastor, a famous Christian author, or one of the well-known personalities on Christian radio or television. You do.

You may speak through your local weekly newspaper, a local radio station, or you may someday be called upon to join a group of experts on *Meet the Press*. But you're the one who will speak for Christianity in America.

My contention is that not many of us have been speaking. Very few of us ever consider ways we could engage our culture with views that have been shaped by the transforming message of the Gospel. And because of that, Christian thought and values are missing from American culture.

If no one in your community is speaking for Christians in the public arena, your community will grow increasingly secular and even anti-Christian. Maybe it's time for you to start roaring.

> Whatever happens, conduct yourselves in a manner worthy of the gospel of Christ.
>
> Philippians 1:27

4

The Movies: Box Office Closed

The movies have made me a better person.

I really believe this. As it was with many who grew up in the forties and fifties, in those halcyon pre-television days, movies were a big part of my life. My mother was and is a true fan of the silver screen, and, since I was an only child, the two of us would take in several movies a week during my early childhood. We often had to sell milk bottles and soft-drink bottles to get bus fare and the price of two tickets, but many summer afternoons found us escaping the Texas heat in a cool, dark theater, often enjoying that bygone two-for-one bargain known as a double feature. There were even some days, much to my father's chagrin, that my mother and I would take in two double features in an afternoon—four full-length motion pictures, plus "selected short subjects" in one day!

Not only did Mom and I see many movies during the week, my father almost always took the three of us to a Friday night movie. Hamburgers, followed by a movie on Friday evening, was as close to being a ritual in my family as anything. It was, unfortunately, much more regular than church on Sunday. Because I saw so many movies as a youngster, I can relive much of my childhood through old flicks on television. And, as I said, I believe I am a better person because of the movies. In those days, almost every movie extolled virtue. Good triumphed over evil. There were absolutes. There were real heroes.

Respect for women was lauded. Courage, bravery, and sacrifice were qualities to be praised. Love of country was promoted. Helping the underdog was shown to be a noble pursuit. True romance, extolling fidelity and loyalty, was almost the essence of the movies of that era. Family life was depicted favorably, even idealized. Education was shown as a prize to be sought. Even love for and kindness to animals were regular movie themes.

God, the church, and those who worked for the church were never demeaned, though they usually were not drawn too clearly. And, once in awhile, the big screen was used to bring powerful messages of God and even of Jesus Christ. Certainly, *King of Kings* and *The Robe* were the first real, meaningful presentations of Christ and His message that ever impacted my life. I really believe that it was because of those movies that I was more open and objective when the claims of Christ were presented to me from Scripture. The movies of my childhood really did make me a better person.

Then something strange happened. At age thirteen I was attracted (through sports) to a small church nearby, and almost immediately I was cut off from the movies. All movies. Even the basically wholesome movies described above were anathema to this church and were all but forbidden to its members. The winsomeness of the church people and of the Christ preached in their church convinced me "to buy the whole package" and so, reluctantly, I virtually gave up the movies for most of my teenage and college years. (It is ironic that now, with the movies almost indescribably worse in terms of values they project, this same denomination and its institutions have no hard and fast rules relative to attending the cinema, and most of its members are, one presumes, regular ticket buyers.)

Even though I was cut off from regular Hollywood fare, the big screen continued to demonstrate its attraction and power for me during my teenage years. In those days, Billy Graham and his organization were producing quality dramatic motion pictures conveying a gospel message. And they were giving these pictures significant distribution. Most were shown in regular theaters, using the best available sound and projection equipment. When a new Billy Graham picture opened in town, it was a big deal, particularly for the young people of a church that forbade them to go to Hollywood movies. To take a girl to the premiere of a Billy Graham film was the biggest date of the year for many Christian teenagers. In addition, many churches used the attractiveness of these films as one of their major evangelistic outreaches. The idea, and a good one, was for church members to invite their friends, who might never go with them to church, to have a night out with them at the movies. In the neutral setting of a movie theater, a quality motion picture would present the claims of Christ in a dramatic way. It was a good idea.

Unfortunately, Billy Graham's motion picture efforts came at a time when there was no after-market in television and/or videocassette distribution available to either extend the reach or help defray the production costs. It has now been many years since the last Graham film was released. And, more unfortunately, even tragically, Graham's efforts were the last regular quality effort of the church to use this powerful, important, uniquely American medium to bring the salt of the Gospel to the world. There are now almost no lambs roaring in Hollywood and anything close to a Christian message or theme rarely appears on the screens of the thousands of movie theaters across the country. The Christian church, which had some time ago abandoned the motion picture industry as a place of ministry and outreach, now, for all practical purposes, abandoned the medium itself as a way to communicate the message of Christ to the world at large.

When the church and its people are absent, when there is no preserving salt and no roaring lambs, the same thing always happens. It is just as sure as a law of physics. When a vacuum is created, it is always filled. When good departs, evil always fills in behind it. If you remove the salt, the meat spoils. It rots. This is what happened to the movies. To think that my children and grandchildren could be better people by ingesting a steady diet of movies today the way I did as a child would be ludicrous. Once again, Christians left the scene, and, again, the scene was an important one. The movies continue to play a big part in how America thinks and in what the world thinks about America. The power of the silver screen is still there, but it is just not a power for good and right.

Michael Medved, the respected movie critic, host of *Sneak Preview* on PBS, and author of the recently released *Hollywood vs. America*, says that there is a definite antireligion bias in Hollywood. In his now-famous lecture at Hillsdale College, Medved cited many instances when movie makers went out of their way, i.e., spent lots of their own money, to blast religion and religious values. To make his point, he noted that almost none of the really religiously offensive films did anything but lose money for their producers. These include such notorious bombs as *The Last Temptation of Christ, Monsignor, Agnes of God, The Runner*

Stumbles, True Confessions, Mass Appeal, and *The Mission.* By contrast, films that in many ways conveyed a positive look at religion and religious values found large audiences and made much more money. Those cited include *Chariots of Fire, Tender Mercies, The Trip to Bountiful, Witness,* and *A Cry in the Dark.* Medved concludes that the moguls in Hollywood are so biased against religious values that they are ready to put significant amounts of money behind their beliefs. He says,

> Why hasn't Hollywood gotten the message? The one thing this industry is supposed to be able to do is to read the bottom line. Why, then, do savvy producers continue to authorize scores of projects that portray religious leaders as crazed conspiratorial charlatans, when similar films have failed so conspicuously in the past?
>
> It is hard to escape the conclusion that there is a perverse sort of idealism at work here. For many of the most powerful people in the entertainment business, hostility to traditional religion goes so deep and burns so intensely that they insist on expressing that hostility even at the risk of commercial disaster.

In this context, Medved cites the 1985 *King David* production, which cost $28 million to produce and attracted less than $3 million in ticket sales. This film advanced the totally unsupported conclusion that the biblical king rejected God at the end of his life. Medved gives this account of an interview he conducted on the film:

> A few weeks before the film's release, one of the people who created it spoke to me proudly of its "fearless integrity." "We could have gone the easy way and played to

the Bible belt," he said, "but we wanted to make a tough, honest film. We don't see David as a gung-ho, Praise-the-Lord kind of guy. We wanted to make him a richer, deeper, character." In his mind, in other words, secure religious faith is incompatible with depth of character.

For our purposes here, the most germane and compelling words of Medved's powerful lecture are these: "It's easy for most movie makers to assume a patronizing attitude toward religiously committed people because they know so few of them personally. If most big-screen images of religious leaders tend to resemble Swaggart or Bakker, it's because evangelists on television are the only believers who are readily visible to the members of the film colony." (Interested readers can obtain a complete copy of Medved's lecture by writing to Imprimis, Hillsdale College, Hillsdale, Michigan 49242. It is an important document and well worth having).

What Medved is saying is that since there are so few Christians in the Hollywood film industry, can we blame the moviemakers for their errors when they try to portray religious faith? We've left the interpretation of our faith, our church, and our Savior up to non-Christians. Is it their fault if they almost always get it wrong? Is it their fault if Swaggart and Bakker are the primary models they have for Christian characters in their films? The answer, I believe, is obvious. We left, and the world is paying a significant price for our abdication.

Remember, twenty million people go to the movies each week in America alone. Millions more see movies on television and cassettes. Only very rarely do they see anything that points them to Christ. Our fault.

Typically, but unfortunately, our response to the sacrilege and blasphemy of modern movies is to whine, demonstrate, boycott, and keep score. Again, as with television, we have almost no alternatives to offer. We cannot say, "Don't watch that trash. Watch this film of a great story that is uplifting and ennobling." We can't say that, because we haven't produced those films in any numbers. Basically, we are saying to the twenty million who attend movies every week: "Stay home. But don't watch television, because we haven't produced anything there either." This is not a logically defensible position. It won't play, not even in Peoria.

Again, all too typically, it seems that one of our few responses to a very bad situation is not to provide good alternatives but to spend our time, energies, and the Lord's money in scorekeeping operations. A recent newspaper column had this account: "Several times a week, Movie Morality Ministries sends reviewers into theaters to count cuss words, bare breasts, axe murders and assorted other Hollywood favorites." From Movie Morality Ministries, we learn that the "F" word is used fifty-eight times in *JFK*. I feel sure the people of this "ministry" feel they are serving God in their hearts and that people who contribute to their cause feel they have done their Christian duty relative to the movies. This, no doubt, makes them feel active and engaged as Christians where the movies are concerned. I could be wrong, but I do not think this is the kind of thing Christ meant when he said, "You will be my witnesses in Jerusalem, and in all Judea and Samaria, and to the ends of the earth" (Acts 1:8). And frankly, I don't think it takes a cadre of movie monitors to deduce that movies are in pretty bad shape.

Because we have been absent so long, Hollywood may be the uttermost part of the earth, more foreign in many ways than China, India, or Africa as far as the Gospel is concerned. Still, we are commanded to go there and be witnesses, and you can't witness without being present. Christians need to be in Hollywood, working along-side the men and women who are producing the movies that twenty million people see each week. What a mission field!

It has been years since *Chariots of Fire*, with its evocative theme song, its compelling story, and its fair and sympathetic depiction of a Christian character, sneaked into movie theaters around the world. "Sneaked" is the right way to describe its emergence. Because of its Best Picture Academy Award and the classic status it has now achieved, it is important to remember that *Chariots of Fire* was a "small" movie, relatively very inexpensive to produce and with no important, big-name stars among its principal play-ers. Only word-of-mouth publicity kept it alive at the box office. It was quietly released and had to win its way by the quality of the production and subsequent response of the viewers. Obviously, it succeeded extraordinarily well.

Naïve soul that I am, I believed that the success of *Chariots* would trigger a spate of similar films. It seemed to me that the movie moguls would see that a great, uplifting story, competently acted, backed up by stirring music and produced on a reasonable budget could be a formula for success after success. It was not to be. There have been few if any *Chariots* to follow the original. I wanted to find out why.

To find out why, I spoke with David Puttnam, the creator and producer of *Chariots*. The worldwide success of his great movie and the Best Picture Oscar it earned catapulted Puttnam into perhaps the most powerful position in the motion picture industry. He became the head of Columbia Pictures, then owned by Coca-Cola. His tenure there was a stormy one. The Hollywood establishment fought him at every turn and ridiculed his common-sense approach to movie making. The moguls and mavens won and Puttnam soon returned to London, chastened and defeated. I wanted to visit with him and hear firsthand why the success of *Chariots* could not, or at least had not, been replicated.

Getting in touch with Puttnam required a good deal of detective work, and I finally had to go through ex-baseball commissioner, Fay Vincent, who once represented Coca Cola in running Columbia Pictures making him, in effect, Puttnam's boss. Through Fay's good help a date was set for me to meet Puttnam in his difficult-to-find London office. It was almost as if he wanted to get as far away from the glitz and glamour of Hollywood as possible. His small space was tucked away in an old mews in an obscure section of London. The entire building that it was in probably did not contain the area of his magnificent suite of offices at Columbia.

A large, bearded man, Puttnam was initially cool but courteous. He was probably wary of yet another American there to interview him about *Chariots*, his tenure at Columbia, and the aftermath. Sports soon provided a common ground for us. His father had been a sportswriter on a London paper, and we discovered we had friends and acquaintances in common. We had an animated conversation about the difference between a baseball pitcher and a cricket bowler. I enjoyed myself with him.

When the discussion turned to *Chariots* and to why there had been so few quality pictures following it, Puttnam turned melancholy. It was obvious that he was looking for the next *Chariots*. His office sort of overflowed with scripts in various stages of being read. He was looking, but not finding. He said that there were just no good scripts being brought to him. He said it with sadness. Here was a guy who, based on his previous track record, could certainly raise the money to produce any movie he wanted to make. He had shown an affinity for producing quality, uplifting, affirming, even Christian-oriented movies, but no one was bringing him scripts of quality. I couldn't help but wonder where the Christian screenwriters were. David Puttnam, sitting in his little out-of-the-way office in London, is an untapped resource for people who care about quality movies. To tap the resource, the church needs writers. We have the Movie Morality Ministries to keep score for us, but we do not have the writers to change the score in our favor.

Although it was difficult to arrange the time with David Puttnam, God has given me a close, warm relationship with one of the legendary giants of the movie industry.

Martin Jurow lives in my home town of Dallas, Texas. Although physically a small man, his heart, intellect, and reservoir of goodwill are huge. His experience in and knowledge of the movie business are unsurpassed, encyclopedic. He has produced such classics as *The Pink Panther, Breakfast at Tiffany's,* and *Terms of Endearment,* among many others. He has known all the great stars and directors and all the important studio executives. Great writers for the movies, such as Louis L'Amour, were among his close personal friends. To spend time with Martin is akin to having lunch at the MGM commissary in the era of the great stars of the studio system. As he talks, the stars seem to materialize and pass by as if passing by your lunch table. He is a superb raconteur.

Martin has always been very generous in giving me time. He invited me to his home near the Southern Methodist University campus, where he teaches a tremendously popular course on the business of entertainment. After we spent some time deploring the dearth of quality in current movies and he shared with me his anger in not being able to be comfortable with his wife and daughter in most movies he now sees, we began to talk about alternatives.

If a group of caring people would develop a great script with a biblical message, I asked him, could such a movie be produced and distributed? I wanted to know whether, even with all the antipathy to religion cited by Michael Medved, it was still possible to make and distribute quality movies with a message. His reply sort of stunned me. Almost with vehemence he said, "Of course they could! It isn't that it can't be done; it's that nobody tries." We have not, because we ask not.

He illustrated his point with a story. The wife of a Methodist minister knew of a story she believed should be made into a film. This woman, unlike most of us, acted on her belief. Knowing that one of the legendary film makers lived in the same city, she picked up the phone and called Martin. She asked if he would help her produce a movie. His reply was, "Of course I will!" We receive not, because we ask not. The unlikely partnership of a Dallas minister's wife and a Hollywood legend produced a wonderful result. Because a preacher's wife saw, through eyes of faith, the possibility of putting a great story on the big screen and because people of good will, such as Martin Jurow, often respond to others of good will, we have *Papa Was a Preacher*. My wife and I had the great joy of seeing this wonderful full-length motion picture in one of our local theaters. It was up there on the big screen just as any other production would be. The difference is that it presents an honest, humorous, sympathetic picture of the life of a Protestant clergyman and his family. It does not present them as perfect; it presents them as committed to the cause of Christ and caring about the welfare of others. And, because it is on film, many generations of people will be able to see it in many different mediums, in many different venues. I am thrilled to be able to write about this great example of active faith, of salt delivered, of a lamb that roared, roared with a sound as sweet as can be. If you haven't seen this movie, rent it tonight.

After telling me about *Papa Was a Preacher*, Martin gave me a formula for replicating its success. Maybe there's someone out there—maybe a group of Christian businessmen and creative types who will give this formula a try. Here are the salient points:

1. Select a quality story with a sound message and appealing characters.
2. Develop a sensible budget. The script should not call for special effects or expensive stunts, car chases, etc. (The budget for *Papa Was a Preacher* was about $2.5 million.)
3. Spread the risk. No single person put more than fifty thousand dollars into *Papa Was a Preacher*. Bring people to the project who see it as a mission, not as an investment. If the film is a financial success, this should be seen as a bonus.
4. Build a relationship with a distributor who specializes in "small" quality movies.
5. Have a European strategy. American films are much more in demand in Europe than they are in America. Films made only for television distribution in America are often given significant theatrical distribution in Europe.
6. Have an after-market strategy. Unlike the days when Billy Graham produced his movies, there is today a very dynamic market for films beyond their original intended use. There is at least cable television distribution (more about this later) available on almost any quality film, and, more and more, video-cassette distribution both extends the reach and produces revenues for films.
7. Do not be afraid to go after a quality cast. Actors, even the best, most of them highly paid, want to work and want to do quality work. They will often agree to do roles of quality at rates far, far below their usual fees. Examples of this are Robert Duval in *Tender Mercies* (for which he won an Oscar), Geraldine Page in *A Trip to Bountiful* (for which she won an

Oscar), and Sir John Gielgud in *Chariots of Fire*, in which he performed an important cameo role.

Martin feels that any denomination or group of Christians (*Papa Was a Preacher* was financed by the members of one suburban Dallas church) could make the above strategy work over and over again if there were people developing quality scripts. (You are by now probably tired of my saying, "The church needs writers." But it is true, and it needs emphasizing.)

Christians can take heart in the knowledge that *Papa Was a Preacher* is not the only recent success of Christian film makers.

Frank Schroeder provides an inspiring example of persistence and perseverance and, perhaps, another example of how to go about recapturing some of the lost ground in the motion picture business. While working in a sports television ministry (a man after my own heart!) he became convinced that a motion picture should be made on the life of basketball legend "Pistol" Pete Maravich, who had come to faith in Christ late in his career. Even the untimely death of Maravich himself did not deter Schroeder. Taking a page from the *Papa Was a Preacher* story, he raised the $2 million production budget from a group of private Christian investors and completed *The Pistol: Birth of a Legend.* Once he had the film, he could not find either a distributor or the money to distribute the film himself. He decided on a unique approach to raising the distribution dollars. He would sell a corporate sponsor an on-screen promotion—in effect, a commercial message to be shown as a lead-in each time the movie would be shown in a theater. Fifty-five corporations turned him down before the Atlanta based fast-food chain Chick-fil-A agreed to cover the marketing cost of the film in exchange for the on-screen promotion. A smart, synergistic adjunct was that the film would also be promoted in the 435 Chick-fil-A restaurants across the country.

Even with the marketing dollars at last in hand, Schroeder still faced a very high hurdle. He needed to persuade movie theater owners that audiences would accept a film with a commercial lead-in. Most large theater chains wouldn't even consider it. By convincing executives of General Cinema, the nation's third-largest theater chain, to at least view the film and the Chick-fil-A lead-in, he scored a breakthrough. GC agreed to play it, and other major chains followed.

With faith, determination, the help of Christian friends and Christian businesses, Frank Schroeder succeeded in producing and distributing a quality film with a solid Christian message. I am sure this is no big deal to him, but he also immediately gained entry into my Roaring Lambs Hall of Fame.

Following the successful theatrical release, *Pistol* was picked up by Sony for home-video distribution. This kind of success has enabled Schroeder to put four more quality films into development, including the final two in the *Pistol* trilogy. He is opening up the box office. I hope Schroeder's success thrills you as much as it does me. But what should individual Christians do in response to Schroeder's heroics? Well, first of all, buy a Chick-fil-A sandwich. It's a great sandwich! Perhaps, more than that, we should show the Christian-oriented companies such as Chick-fil-A that we applaud their strategic thinking, which synergistically combines sound business sense with an effort to tell The Story.

Second, watch for Frank Schroeder films. If one comes to your city, buy a ticket. Go see it. Take a friend who needs to see a quality presentation of the gospel message.

Third, if you are an investor or have means to contribute to God's work here on earth, consider putting money into Schroeder's films.

However, the very best thing you can do for Frank Schroeder is to help him find great stories and encourage Christian writers to consider writing screenplays for him.

Believe me, I'm dead serious about this business of cleaning up movies by joining rather than fighting the industry. Think of all the effort that has gone into boycotting and slamming the admittedly awful movies being produced today. Are we better off for it? Can you honestly say you've noticed that this strategy is working? Are you pleased with the general fare offered in movie theaters today? Let's be honest: all our protests have done is make us feel good about standing up and being counted. They have not cleaned up Hollywood, nor will they. The studios just don't care. What will ultimately speak to them is profit. Sure, they may be willing to lose money to make a few perverted films, but by and large the producers want to make money. If done right, good, clean, uplifting, even faith-affirming movies will make it to the silver screen.

Let me close this chapter, then, with just two more examples. If I told you that the Kuntz brothers are not particularly impressive people at first sight, it would not be a pejorative statement. In fact, it is a high compliment. These rather ordinary guys operating out of very modest offices with no big corporate dollars and no big-time Hollywood connections have accomplished extraordinary things. They have made movies, successful movies, all with a Christian message. The key to their success has been in identifying and attracting a star who sees and identifies with the mission they have undertaken. *Dakota*, their most recent production, gained acceptance into movie theaters mainly because of its young star, Lou Diamond Phillips. The Kuntz brothers spotted this compelling young actor before he had become the big star he was destined to be and signed him on for their film. It was one of those roaring-lamb kinds of deals that will have eternal benefits for the kingdom.

I don't want to leave the impression that, even with a Lou Diamond Phillips, the Kuntz brothers had it easy. To get *Dakota* produced and distributed took the same kind of determination and dedication that Frank Schroeder has. It took the entire Kuntz family—wives, children, friends, neighbors—and it took at least two years of all their lives. Was it worth it? Before you decide, let me tell you about the greatest success of *Dakota*.

Earlier I mentioned the large number of cable channels now available as "after-market" distribution for films. Well, the Kuntz brothers hit a cable channel home run with *Dakota*. They made a deal for their movie with Home Box Office—HBO—the country's premium movie channel. HBO, the channel the blasters and boycotters love to hate. HBO, where you can catch some of the worst Hollywood has to offer, but also *Dakota*, which is the story of a Christian family who live out their faith by befriending a young rebel played by Lou Diamond Phillips and help him to see that Christ is the answer to his alienation. More than a year after its debut on the channel, HBO continues to air *Dakota*. Millions continue to see it. Because of the vision of Darryl and Frank Kuntz there is a roar of the lambs on HBO. And the roar will be long and loud, for *Dakota* will be available on videocassette for years to come. It is certain that many young people, attracted by Lou Diamond Phillips, will see it.

Was it worth it? It was eternally worth it, and the Kuntz brothers occupy a place of honor in my mythical Roaring Lambs Hall of Fame. More important, they have provided a model for the rest of us as to how ordinary people can do extraordinary things with God's help. Isn't this a better way to "fight" Hollywood?

Finally, I'd like to tell you about Rhonda Richards, a talented producer for my own company, ProServ Television. As a graduate of Greenville College, which is also my alma mater, Rhonda has already in her young life demonstrated that what I'm talking about in this book is no pipe dream. Rhonda has not let the fact that she attended a small Christian college deter her from her goal. An English major in college, she could easily have followed a traditional path toward high school teaching. Nothing wrong with that. But Rhonda had other ideas, different ideas. She wanted to produce movies. I am sure many people told her that women from small Christian colleges don't produce movies. If she heard discouraging words, they did not deter her. Almost totally on her own, she obtained admission and a fellowship to study at the prestigious Stanford University film school. Before coming to PSTV, she had already earned an on-screen credit for her work on Kevin Costner's epic, *Dances With Wolves*. Seeing her name roll by on the credits of this important film is more exciting to me than the buffalo hunt, the battle scenes, or Costner's escape from his captors. The next time you see *Dances With Wolves* on television or on vidcocassette, watch the credits. Watch for Rhonda Richards' name. Let this be both an encouragement and a challenge. Let it be evidence that Christians who want to change Hollywood from the inside can at least have a chance. Let it be convincing to all of us who have deserted the movies.

My prayer is that Rhonda will fully realize her opportunities and responsibilities and will help put the most important story of all up on the big screen many times for many to see. I hope her example will inspire many others.

The movies, the people who make them, and the people who see them are important. The absence of God's people from the movies has been tragic. Millions of people are being misled and corrupted because the salt has been absent and because the lambs have not roared. A reentry for Christians presents very formidable challenges, but God is able if his people are obedient. The movies can be both an important mission field and an important vehicle for the gospel message.

We need to focus on the individual heroics of the minister's wife who has given us *Papa Was a Preacher*, on what Frank Schroeder and the Kuntz brothers have been able to accomplish, on the insight and commitment of executives such as those at Chick-fil-A, on the potential of our young people like Rhonda Richards, and on the available resources represented by men of good will such as Martin Jurow and David Puttnam.

Think what these people have accomplished on their own. Now think what could be accomplished if God's people in America would begin to think strategically about the movies and about the twenty million souls who attend them each week. If churches, Christian businessmen, Christian colleges, Christian foundations, and Christian writers would begin to prayerfully target the movies, I have no doubt that we could hang a welcome sign on the box offices of America, signifying that, once again, the movies are a place and a medium in which God is honored. Let's do it.

> Do your best to present yourself to God as one approved, a workman who does not need to be ashamed and who correctly handles the word of truth.
>
> 2 Timothy 2:15

5

Television: Fade to Black

The most compelling of all the recently introduced network television programs is the CBS series *Brooklyn Bridge*. It is the work of Gary David Goldberg, the fine writer/producer who created *Family Ties* and made Michael J. Fox a star. *Brooklyn Bridge*, wonderfully cast, brilliantly written and beautifully photographed, takes viewers inside a Jewish family living in Brooklyn, New York, in the late forties and early fifties. After watching only a few episodes, you begin to get a deeper understanding of, and a more real appreciation for, many things Jewish.

Northern Exposure is one of the most innovative, as well as one of the most critically acclaimed, new television series of the past several years. It chronicles the unlikely adventures of a young Jewish doctor, who surprisingly finds himself practicing in an isolated Alaskan frontier town. And, although played more for laughs than *Brooklyn Bridge*, it provides insights and understanding into how American Jews relate to a different kind of American culture.

Another recent runaway hit has been *Murphy Brown*, the Candice Bergen vehicle set in the news department of a fictitious television network. Among the most appealing of the continuing characters in the show is Miles Silverberg, the Jewish executive producer of the weekly news program starring the Murphy Brown character. Again, played strongly for laughs, the Silverberg character nevertheless gives viewers continuing insights into the life and thinking of a Jew in America.

The obvious point is that American television viewers have many opportunities to see finely drawn and sympathetically presented Jewish characters on a regular basis. *Brooklyn Bridge, Northern Exposure*, and *Murphy Brown* are only examples of some of the more recent programs with well-defined Jewish characters. There have been many others. Jewish lawyers, policemen, housewives, teachers, and even taxi drivers have long populated our television landscape. While some might argue that many of these characters contribute to a stereotype of Jews, nonetheless the treatment is generally kind. We may laugh, but not in derision or ridicule.

On the other hand, there is not a single dramatic program currently on network television, and none within memory, that attempts to delineate the life of a Protestant Christian in America. There is no sitcom, no courtroom drama, no Western, no police story with identifiable Christian characters. There are approximately six million Jews in America and at least fifty million Protestant Christians. Something is wrong.

What is wrong has nothing to do with American Jews. Not only do I honor them collectively as a covenant people of God, I admire the way they have entered the mainstream of American culture. Where television is concerned, people who are Jewish have taken their identities with them as they moved into this influential medium. It would be unfair and incorrect to say that the networks are favorable to Jews. Instead, people in the industry who are Jewish have not tried to hide who they are. We who are Christians need to learn from this. We've had it wrong from the beginning and have never caught up.

Unlike innovations in printing, which Christians powerfully co-opted for good to spread God's Word, television was regarded from the first with suspicion and antipathy. Too many of us saw this morally neutral technology as somehow inherently evil. In my own denomination some of our more radically conservative conferences actually sponsored events in the early fifties at which television sets were smashed. Many preached against the evil of having "Satan's black box" in one's living room. Even though most Christians did not go to these extremes, neither did the church catch a vision of what television could do as a means of building God's kingdom. The kingdom has suffered ever since.

Now we face a very formidable uphill task. Television is a moral catastrophe, with indecency being the norm. But even in this arena that is so influential we must become roaring lambs. We cannot continue to abdicate our responsibilities. We must have a strategy that will allow us to build some beachheads and then to expand those in order to use television to bring a Christian perspective to the living rooms of America.

I believe it's possible to bring Christian values into television, but it won't happen through strident public criticism and boycotts. Even if the criticism and boycotts were effective in reducing sex and violence on television, which they are not, they still do not bring any positive alternatives to the medium. The best thing a boycott can do is cause television to "fade to black" to use industry parlance, to have television screens with no picture and no sound. Is this any way to change television?

The television producer who seems to be most opposed by the boycotters is Norman Lear, the creator of *All in the Family*, and many other prime-time programs. While we protest, boycott, and wring our hands, Lear produces and distributes programs. Who do you think is winning the battle for the hearts and minds of America?

It is very unfortunate that the only efforts organized by Christians to affect mainstream television have been negative and reactionary. I feel sure that Rev. Donald Wildmon and his group, which spends its time monitoring network television broadcasts, holding press conferences, denouncing the evils of network programming, organizing boycotts of the products of program sponsors, and raising funds from well-meaning Christians, are themselves well meaning. The facts are, however, that their efforts do a significant disservice to the cause of Christ relative to television.

First of all, not only are their efforts unsuccessful, they are really not taken seriously inside the industry. A sort of bemused lip service is given to their complaints as the easiest way to deal with them. (In many ways, the cause of Christ is hurt most, not when it is vigorously denounced and fought against, but when it is laughed at and not taken seriously.) Although they announce an occasional success in getting an advertiser to pull support from a particular program, no real positive change in programming is ever effected. Violence, explicit sex, and sexual innuendo continue to proliferate as do other objectionable plots and characters.

Second, most methods of attacking television inevitably result in charges of censorship being leveled against us. In twentieth-century America, this is a very difficult charge to defend against and results in an uphill battle. In it we are always so busy trying to explain that we are not really in favor of censorship, that we never get around to explaining who Christ is or why He came. The enemy always occupies the high ground.

The third, and perhaps the most damaging disservice the blasters and boycotters do to the cause of Christ as it relates to television is that it distracts Christians and drains financial support from any positive effort to bring the real salt of the Gospel to bear on the medium. It gives Christians an easy way out. It is possible for well-meaning Christians to make a financial contribution in support of Donald Wildmon's boycotts or Jerry Falwell's denunciation campaign against television and feel that they have done all that's required and have made a real contribution to the kingdom. All they have done is wasted the Lord's money.

I would like to see all the effort, all the mailings, all the organizations, and all the money Wildmon and others use to blast and boycott spent instead in a positive effort to promote good things for television. I suggested in letters to each of them that we develop an awards program to honor the producers, sponsors, and networks who put the best programming on tel evision on the theory, to use the Christopher's slogan, that "it is better to light one candle than it is to curse the darkness." (Their only response was to send more form letters asking for money.) And on the theory that this might encourage more good programming, I would like to see Wildmon and his colleagues at a black-tie dinner in New York handing out awards of appreciation to the chairman of Proctor and Gamble for the good programs they do sponsor rather than calling for a boycott of its products in retaliation for the bad programs they sponsor. I feel sure a full-page ad in the *New York Times* saluting good programs and their sponsors would have a much more positive effect on the medium than do all the denunciations of the bad.

A very positive and beneficial way Wildmon could use the funds he collects from well-meaning Christians across the country would be to use them in an effort to build audiences for quality programs when they are on. There are proven advertising strategies that can significantly increase audience ratings. I would like to see funds used to promote quality programs because, in the end, this would do more to change the medium for good than all the boycotts and all the hand wringing.

From my own experience, let me give you a sad example of what happens when the church is so distracted by efforts to stamp out evil that it forgets to cooperate with efforts to produce good.

Time Warner is the largest media company in America. Their Home Box Office is far and away the most successful and influential of the pay cable services sending programming into America's homes via satellite.

One day in New York I was in the office of one of the two very able men who control HBO programming. These are not religious men, but they are men of great good will. I was pitching a program with an obvious Christian message. Before I got very deep into my presentation, my friend stopped me and said, "That's not something we would put on HBO. You need to go downstairs and meet Mack Perryman, who will be running our new Festival Channel. He is a born-again Christian, and we are going to launch this new service, which will carry only family programming."

Needless to say, I could not get downstairs fast enough. It was extremely exciting to think that a powerhouse such as HBO would be starting a new programming service to be run by a "born-again Christian." I met Mack and we began to talk about our faith and to discuss the kind of programs Festival would carry. It would be a sort of "faith and values" channel. It would carry quality movies for the whole family and other programming that would promote family values. It would be an answer to many people's prayers.

Festival, even with all the HBO and TIME resources behind it, did not get off the ground. It was a programming service run by a Christian and designed for Christians and other members of the so-called Moral Majority, but they could never get Christians to rally around and support it. Even in "Bible Belt" test markets it received scant support. A very great opportunity was lost because the church in America was so busy denouncing something bad that it could not be bothered to support something really good.

Again, the salt that Christ commands us to be calls for much more than negativism. It calls for penetration through positive alternatives that convey the message of the Gospel. Where television is concerned, getting involved the right way will not be easy. It's much easier to organize boycotts and distribute pamphlets telling us how bad television programming is (something we already know). Producing and distributing positive, God-honoring programming is hard, but that is really the only way to bring real salt to television. It's the only way to be a roaring lamb.

Television must be seen as a long-range project for the church. Because we have such a late start, gains will come slowly and at a price, but we must begin. With God's help, we can bring the preserving salt, even to this very difficult area.

The place to begin is with programs, and programs begin with writing. Television is a visual medium, but it begins with the written word. Until a program is down on paper, it cannot make it to the screen. Therefore the most powerful and influential people in the television industry are writers. They are referred to as producers, but they are really writers. Gary David Goldberg, Norman Lear, Stephen Bochco (*Hill Street Blues, L.A. Law*) and Barney Rosensweig (*Cagney and Lacy*) are all writers. Their writing comes to life on television screens and is spilled into American homes.

We need our own roaring lambs to do the same thing for the ninety-five million television homes in America.

Television needs Christian writers. It needs writers who can develop a dramatic series around courageous inner-city pastors, a sitcom set in the home of a family that is trying to live out the Christian life in the rough and tumble of modern American life, a historical adventure series starring missionaries working in hostile jungles or deserts, documentaries about the great heroes and heroines of the faith. We need writers.

God's church has writers, but they are not writing for television. We need local pastors, Christian colleges, and seminaries to begin to understand this need and to bring their influence and resources to bear on it. Pastors should be sure that the young people in their congregations see writing for television as a worthy calling for Christians. Our colleges must develop much stronger writing programs generally and television writing programs particularly. Some of our Christian colleges have television majors and minors, but all those I am aware of stress production and technology, which is roughly akin to having biblical studies programs stress printing and lithography. The means of production is not a problem for us. We need the words and the Word brought to the television screen. Seminaries, where so many of our most brilliant writers reside, must begin to understand the potential and power of television and must institute programs to develop writers for this ministry.

We also need Christians of wealth and Christian foundations to begin to direct some of their resources to encouraging Christian writing for television. This can be done by endowing programs at colleges and seminaries; by offering prizes, including monetary rewards, for the best scripts or program treatments; by sponsoring television writing workshops; and by guaranteeing production dollars for programs of merit. Christian foundations, wanting to be sure their contributions have maximum kingdom impact, should consider television writing as an area for concentration.

More than anything else, television wants stories—great stories. The Christian church has great stories—is a great story. We need to be telling it through the dynamic medium of television. Wonderful stories, well told and well presented, almost always find their way on to television.

To be fair to the people who control television programming, those who decide what programs get on, almost always are as morally neutral as the technology of television itself. They put on the best they have that people will watch. Advertisers for the most part, pay for the best available programs people will watch. The basic reason there is so much bad programming, so much that is evil and debasing, is that that is all they have from which to choose.

I do not subscribe to the theory that there is some huge secret nefarious organization with headquarters in New York and Hollywood whose goal is to use television to corrupt American society. That kind of organization, that kind of effort, that kind of plot is unnecessary. It is much simpler than that. God's people do not tell their stories. Other people do tell theirs. Television, the morally neutral medium, pumps out what is fed into it. We Christians are not feeding it the great stories of faith, brotherhood, courage, and sacrifice. We have the stories, we know them, but we tell them mostly only to each other. We need to begin using television, the television that reaches the homes of those who have not heard and who do not understand, to tell the stories to those who most need to see and hear. We need Christian television writers.

Again, it will not be easy. But it was and is not easy either to take the Gospel to China, India, and Africa. Men and women of courage, faith, and conviction did it and continue to do it at great sacrifice. Men and women of great skill and dedication translate God's Word into the most difficult of languages. Even where no written language exists, they create one so that God's supreme Story, that of His Son, can be accessible to all. Surely, television, with God's help, can also be reached with His truth. Surely the ninety-five million U.S. television homes provide as needy a field as any in China, India, or Africa. Television provides a formidable challenge for the church, but God is able, and the time to begin is now.

Christian commercial enterprises, particularly those in the communications business (such as the publisher of this book) should begin to develop strategies for impacting mainstream television. They have many of the resources—particularly writers—already at their disposal and lack only a vision of what can be accomplished, both in terms of bottom-line profit and kingdom building. Quality television programming, even with Christian content, can and should be a profitable undertaking. Children's programming and documentaries would be areas in which to begin. With ancillary income from cassette sales to supplement broadcast income, financial risks are greatly reduced. Also, nothing promotes the sale of books like a television program of the same name.

Earlier in this chapter I stressed the need not only for programs of worth but also for distribution tactics that work. Programs and distribution are mutually dependent; one is no good without the other. The very best program imaginable is of no value if it does not reach the viewer. A great new program with no distribution is analogous to a great new Bible, such as, say, the new *Life Application Bible*, sitting by the thousands in warehouses, with no distribution to readers. Programming and distribution are the two priorities for Christians seeking to bring salt to television.

Fortunately, new technologies offer a wider variety of distribution options than ever before. Unfortunately, our own reputation as Christians seems to fight against us to keep us from using the medium of television. Let me illustrate.

Bill and Gloria Gaither, the song writers and performers who have created much of the new music most loved by modern American Christians, are also master impresarios. Among their classiest productions is "Jubilate," a New Year's Eve extravaganza of high-energy, star-packed Christian entertainment presented with huge portions of patriotic fervor and staged with flare and panache. Appreciative fans pack Atlanta's Omni arena, adding to the electricity of the evening. The headliners are "crossover" stars, entertainers who have followings in both Christian and secular music—Sandi Patti, Bebe and Cici Winans, Take Six, Carmen, and many others.

It seemed that this would be a perfect New Year's Eve television program for an America with a rekindled sense of patriotism, a country that at last seems to be taking seriously the problems of drinking while driving, and where the only scheduled New Year's Eve television program featured a sort of drunken bacchanal. It seemed "Jubilate" would be nearly perfect "counter" programming. It seemed even more nearly perfect when Coca Cola expressed interest in on-air sponsorship. Programmatically, we had all the ingredients—big stars, classy production, an appreciative and energized live audience, a scheduling rationale (New Year's Eve), no similar program scheduled against it, and interest from prestigious sponsors. Even with all this, our company could not get the program on the air. We could not get distribution. And let me say here that we are not rookies in television distribution. For the past twenty years we have made much of our living through our ability to find a way to get programs distributed. With

"Jubilate" we were not able to overcome the notion that Christians don't watch quality TV.

The main over-the-air networks—ABC, CBS, and:BY NBC—do not:BN believe that Christians in America are an identifiable, reliable audience. They do not believe that Christians will coalesce around programs with obvious Christian content in sufficient numbers to make those programs viable. Their view is that Christians protest against bad programs but watch them anyway and do not watch "religious" programs. They had no interest in "Jubilate."

We next moved to Turner Broadcasting. "Jubilate" was being staged in Atlanta, Turner's home, and in a building, the Omni, which they control. They, too, had no interest.

Our next move was to the Pat Robertson controlled Family Channel. Disappointingly, the Family Channel would rather air reruns of old network programs such as *The Rifleman* than a live program featuring Christian performers singing Christian music. "Jubilate" was not telecast, illustrating the importance of distribution in an effort to use television as a way to move the salt.

In spite of our failure to find distribution for "Jubilate," there is a wide range of distribution options available, and Christians need to understand how best to make use of them for the sake of the kingdom. Remember, television is a business. Don't expect any television executive to air a program because some group thinks "America needs it." Any program that has strong, measurable potential to draw a large audience will usually find its way onto the airwaves. And despite the general absence of good programs, we should all be encouraged with the small number of writers and producers who are at work in the medium. One of those is one of my personal heroes, Bill Moyers. (Sure, I wish he would hew a little closer to his theologically conservative roots, but he still accomplishes some very positive things.) His one-hour special on the old gospel song "Amazing Grace" is, by itself, enough to put Bill into my Roaring Lambs Hall of Fame. With this special he commandeered a full prime-time hour on PBS, and, for much of the hour, the beautifully simple message of the song, sung by some of the world's great voices, spilled into millions of homes. The sound was sweet indeed.

Bill Moyers provides a wonderful example and many lessons for Christians who seek to use television's powerful technology to bring the salt of the Gospel to the people of America.

First of all, remember that Moyers is basically a writer. That he is also an on-camera talent is really only serendipity. It is his writing skill that gives him such access to television time and to the financial support that makes his programs possible. Again, television needs more Christian writers with talent, commitment, and a vision for how their words on paper can be translated into powerful on-screen messages. Parents, pastors, professors, parishes, and publishers all need to focus on encouraging and producing more and better writers, particularly for television.

Moyers also provides a powerful example in regard to distribution. Remember, the very best program is of little use if it is not made available to the right viewers through the right delivery system. A Moyers program on PBS reaches perhaps a hundred times the number of viewers than a program on one of the religious networks such as ACTS, Trinity, or VISN would. He knows his audience and goes after it.

Some time ago, I wrote to Moyers suggesting that we collaborate on producing some programs for commercial networks or syndication, thus giving him access to a different audience from time to time. He promptly wrote back (unlike the Christian leaders who make a living criticizing TV), saying he thought we were doing a good job with our programs and that he felt the PBS audience was the right one for him. When we came back to earth after his overly generous comments about our programming, we realized he was right about his PBS audience. As Christians desiring to be salt in television, we need to be sure we shoot for the largest, neediest audience available to us. PBS is a delivery system Christians need to begin to utilize.

Bill Moyers provides another instructive example for us in the way he and his sponsor/underwriters advertise, publicize, and promote his programs. They don't spend tens of thousands of dollars on program production and then sit back and hope someone watches. Some weeks before the airing of a Moyers special, you will begin to see stories about it in major national publications, and, in the days immediately preceding the airing, striking "tune in" ads will begin appearing on the television pages of newspapers across the country. He builds his audience.

Another admirable Moyers technique is to stylize and title his programs so as to attract the largest possible audience. He brings the viewers to the program with a provocative title, and then, when he has them, delivers his message. We have tried to emulate his technique in our company. A significant part of our Emmy-winning program, "A Hard Road To Glory," which is a history of black athletes in America, is a segment on Marshall Taylor, a turn-of-the-century world championship cyclist who had a strong Christian testimony. To fill a Thanksgiving weekend programming niche, we produced a program called "Athletes Who Care," which chronicled famous athletes who go to special lengths to make positive contributions to the communities in which they live.

Quite naturally, several cited their commitment to Christ as the reason for their good works. Obviously, we used sports to attract an audience and hoped our "salty" presentations were effective. Our few successes certainly do not measure up to what Bill Moyers is able to do, but we try.

Because so much ultraliberal, even radically left-wing programming is on PBS, most Christians take a very dim view of the network. However, the PBS delivery system itself is philosophically neutral. The reason there is so much on it that is offensive to Christians and so little on it with Christian appeal is that, once again, Christians have not produced programs for the network. Almost every other group in America uses PBS to deliver its message. Christians have not done so with any regularity. Keeping in mind that PBS potentially reaches more American homes than any other delivery system—more than either ABC, CBS, or NBC—and has an highly educated, affluent audience base—people who rarely are impacted by the Gospel—we cannot afford to neglect it.

Nothing is easy on television. It is, however, easier to place programs on PBS than on any other delivery system of comparable size. Remember, PBS stands for Public Broadcasting Service, and Congress set it up so that many publics can have access to it. We Christians have just not made very good use of it.

Every local PBS station provides access to the network. A well-produced program on virtually any subject can be distributed to all the PBS stations through any local station. And nothing prevents program producers from going directly to individual PBS stations to promote their programs. There are also regional PBS programming services that will make programs available to all the country's PBS stations. PBS and its member stations have an insatiable desire for programming for which they do not have to pay. Christians should be supplying this programming as a part of the saline solution.

Here's my plan for the church to develop roaring lambs in television:

1. We should put our best writers to work developing quality programs for PBS distribution. These should be documentary programs, whose titles should have broad appeal. They should deliver the gospel message.

2. As Moyers has done, we should develop relationships with steady sources of production dollars for Christian programs on PBS. In the parlance of PBS, they are called underwriters. They can be commercial corporations that gain valuable exposure by their association with PBS programming. Certainly, there are corporations in America who would want to have their name and message associated with well-produced programs carrying intellectually cogent Christian messages. If the publisher of this book were to underwrite a PBS program, here is the kind of exposure it would receive: The Zondervan corporate logo would appear on the screen and an announcer's voice would say, "This program is being brought to you by Zondervan Publishing House of Grand Rapids, publishers of Bibles and quality Christian books for more than one hundred years." Underwriters of the kind of PBS programming we have in mind are in no way limited to religiously oriented companies such as Zondervan. Any corporation interested in reaching a quality audience with quality programs could be an underwriter. We need to cultivate them.

   Regular PBS viewers will be aware that much of the programming on the network is underwritten by foundations. American foundations that have been specifically formed to help spread a biblical message should be shown the efficacy of funding Christian-oriented programs for PBS.

3. We should be sure that when we have invested Christian time, talent, and treasure in producing a program and distributing it on PBS that we build an audience. As Bill Moyers has done

so effectively, we should be sure that a solid publicity campaign is followed by quality "tune in" advertising in key newspapers. Certainly, we should try to coalesce as much of the American church as possible around these programs.

PBS is by no means the only network Christians should target with their programming. It is only the most obvious one. Certainly, there is no reason why the other major over-the-air networks—ABC, CBS, and NBC—should not also be a part of a long-range saline strategy. They should be. They will be tougher, but no one and no Scripture promised it would be easy. Among other current networks, the Discovery Channel, Arts and Entertainment, and the Disney Channel offer perhaps the best opportunity for distribution of quality programs that could deliver a solid Christian message.

I fully understand the reality that not many reading this chapter will ever write, produce, or distribute a television program. After all, I am in the business every day, and I feel fortunate if we are able to produce one or two programs a year that have at least a few grains of salt sprinkled through the contents. But television is so much a part of all our lives that we all can have a part in trying to improve it, a part in trying to see that at least a thin trickle of decent, God-honoring programs course through the coaxial cable that brings so much into our homes and impacts our lives so directly.

Literally every Christian can have a positive productive role to play in regard to television. Here are a few ideas. They may seem simplistic, but they can have real impact:

1. Watch good programs. Don't watch bad ones. If all the Christians in America would do these two things, television in America would change dramatically for the better. Television responds to one thing—number of viewers. If the church in

America would coalesce around quality programs and eschew the bad ones, television would change for the better.

2. Begin immediately to help your children with their television choices. Begin to train a generation of discriminating viewers.

3. As an individual, express your opinion forcefully, rationally, and with grace about what you like and don't like about television. Your individual voice will carry immeasurably more weight than when it is lumped into some organization's petition. Among the places to which your opinion should go are:

   a. Your local station or cable system bringing a particular program into your home
   b. The national network delivering it
   c. The program sponsors, particularly if there is one predominant sponsor
   d. The production company producing the program
   e. The television critic of your local newspaper
   f. The editor of *TV Guide*

   Remember to be as willing to praise as to pan. An encouraging word can be a powerful force for good.

4. Do everything possible to see that more Christians see television as a ministry, as a mission field demanding a Christian strategy. Discuss with your pastor ways your local church can impart this message, particularly to young people looking for an area in which to serve. If you are a graduate of a Christian college or seminary, ask the president how the school's curriculum relates to training writers for television. If you are aware of Christian foundations, ask them about their giving to impact television with the gospel message. If you are a Christian in business or know people who are, find out how advertising dollars can be made available to support television

programming with Christian content. If you belong to a
denomination, ask about how church funds are spent in the
television area. See if you can encourage them to try to impact
mainstream television for good.

5. Don't waste your money and efforts supporting the blasters
   and boycotters.

6. Pray for every Christian you know who is on the television
   front lines trying, against very formidable odds, to bring a
   godly influence to the medium.

Everyone can truly have a part to play in delivering roaring
lambs for television in America. Again, it will not be easy. But
again, Christ did not command us to be salt in only the easy areas
of life. He did assure us, however, that He would be with us and
would empower us through His Spirit to witness for Him in
Jerusalem, in Judea and Samaria, and in the uttermost parts of the
earth. In many ways television may be the uttermost part for
many of us, but we are commanded to go.

The heavens declare the glory of God; the skies proclaim the work of his hands.

Psalm 19:1

6

Literature: Out of Print

Unless you are a very serious tennis fan, you probably do not remember Jun Kuki and Jan Kamiwasumi. During the decade of the seventies, when tennis was becoming a highly organized, widely televised, and very lucrative sport, Kuki and Kamiwasumi were well-respected, very classy journeymen players on the worldwide circuit. I don't think either ever won a major professional tournament, but they played very good tennis and earned a great deal of prize money. They also added a lot to the appeal of the circuit.

As you have guessed from their names, they are Japanese. In almost every city on the pro tour, the tournaments attracted a group of Japanese fans who would come to the events especially to see and root for Kuki and Kamiwasumi. Most tournaments would get an extra shot of publicity because local newspapers would do a feature on the two players from Japan. The tour might be in London, Paris, Sydney, or Chicago, but it was more attractive and more interesting to tennis fans because of the two Japanese players. They added a lot.

Kuki and Kamiwasumi represented their country very well. They were great sportsmen, always respectful of their opponents and the referees and umpires. They always kept their commitments, showed up on time to play, and played very hard and very well—though of course, they did not always win. In fact, as I said before, they never won a major international professional tournament. Even so, their fellow players, tournament promoters, the tennis press, television networks, and tennis fans all were very happy to have Jun Kuki and Jan Kamiwasumi on the tour, a part of professional tennis.

So far, Kuki and Kamiwasumi were the last two Japanese players to have played the pro tennis tour. No other Japanese players have ever played. The circuit has grown even bigger and more lucrative. The prize money is now in the tens of millions of dollars, with additional millions of endorsement dollars available to the top players. Also, the sport has boomed in Japan. Everyone either plays or wants to play tennis. It is a big sport on television, and there are huge international tournaments in Tokyo. When President Bush goes to Japan, he plays tennis with the Emperor, adding even more glamour and prestige to the sport there. But since the time of Kuki and Kamiwasumi no Japanese players have ventured out to play against the best players in the world on the international tour. Why?

It is simply because tennis has grown so big in Japan and is so lucrative for Japanese players who play only in Japanese tournaments that there is little financial incentive for their best players to go and fight it out with players from all the other countries. As one Japanese player told me, "I can make a million dollars a year and never leave home. Why do I want to fly all over the world to make less money and lose a lot of matches against the Europeans and Americans?"

Obviously, with this kind of attitude, no Japanese player will ever win Wimbledon or the U.S. Open, the most coveted prizes in tennis. No player from Japan will ever be ranked number one in the world. Japan will almost certainly never win the Davis Cup, the major international team competition. Even more sadly, no Kukis or Kamiwasumis will be out there in the great international mix of players, bringing their own very special flavor, adding their own special perspective to the sport. Japan has disappeared from tennis. In their small island country, a great deal of tennis is played. They play each other in all kinds of tournaments in all their own cities. But, outside of Japan, no one ever knows the results. No one knows the names of any of the players. No one knows.

Christian writers are like Japanese tennis players. They once ventured out into the wide world of ideas and put their works in head-to-head competition with those of all other persuasions. Like the Japanese tennis players, they did not win every time. Their books did not always shoot to the top of the best-seller lists. Not everyone was always convinced by their stories that often reflected Christian themes and biblical truth. They didn't win every time, but they made an impact. They delivered the salt. From St. Augustine to John Bunyan, to Harriet Beecher Stowe, to Lew Wallace, to Catherine Marshall, to C. S. Lewis, there have been Christian writers who wrote, not for the church, but for the wider world. They were not so much interested in telling their stories to each other as to those who had not heard or did not believe. And their impact was enormous. Entire societies were changed, the histories of sovereign nations were affected, lives were turned around, all because of these great roaring lambs of literature. In fact, the works of the great Christian writers—those who wrote for the public at large—continue to have impact.

Consider the example of C. S. Lewis. He died in 1963, yet his books are still very widely read. Perhaps even more important is the fact that his life, ideas, and writings are still studied by secular scholars. When a new biography of C. S. Lewis is written, it is big news in the literary world. Non-Christians study the writings of C. S. Lewis every day.

Since Lewis, very few, if any, Christian writers and publishers have taken their work to the wider world outside the church. Christian literature, both fiction and nonfiction, is one of the most ghettoized of all the activities of the church. Like the Japanese tennis players, we have a safe, secure, comfortable "island" on which to pursue our writing and publishing. We compete only against each other. Just as the Japanese tennis players don't care to look across the net at Connors, McEnroe, Edberg, and Becker, Christian writers don't seem to want to compete with Michener, Ludlum, Will, Steele, Francis, and Clancey.

The "island" of Christian writing and publishing is the Christian Booksellers Association and their five thousand member stores. Christian writers have this very large, very comfortable market for their wares. Christian publishers can "target" their advertising and promotion in economically productive ways. Successful Christian authors can do very well with royalties from a CBA best seller and the speaking engagements in churches and other religious settings that ensue. They can appear on Christian radio stations, be reviewed in Christian magazines, and win prestigious awards and prizes without ever getting off the island, without ever leaving the ghetto, but also without taking and applying any of the penetrating salt where it is most needed. Books can be huge best-selling prize winners within the CBA universe and be virtually unheard of outside, where most American readers live and buy their books.

Most large metropolitan newspapers have Sunday literary supplements. In these, new books are reviewed, criticized, and promoted. Ideas from books are discussed and debated. Authors both write and are interviewed. Literary news is chronicled. The bestseller lists of fiction and nonfiction books appear, one list for hardcover and one for paperbacks. Some Sunday papers run parallel lists showing best sellers locally and nationally. The most important and prestigious of these Sunday literary supplements is *The New York Times Book Review*. Every Sunday it runs up to forty pages of material about books and authors. And, of course, a centerpiece each week is the New York Times Best Seller lists. These lists are the standard by which America judges whether or not a book is important.

Christian writers, Christian books, and Christian publishers are for the most part completely absent from the *New York Times Book Review* and other similar literary supplements. The readers of these publications, those Americans most interested in reading, writing, and the world of ideas, do not know that most Christian books even exist. The wonderful Christian writers currently writing are virtually unknown to them. The average American buyer of books never goes into a Christian bookstore and very rarely visits the religion section of the bookstore he does visit. Of even more concern is the fact that there is very little written by Christians for the public at large. Today, most Christian writers write for Christian readers (just as I am doing here).

Perhaps this is a good place to say that one of my favorite activities is to spend time in Christian bookstores. I love to prowl the aisles featuring the books of authors I have come to know and admire through their books. When my wife and I visit other cities, we often spend time in Christian bookstores. It is both enjoyable and a real blessing to browse among the really significant books being written by Christian authors. Ken Gire, Larry Crabb, Chuck Swindoll, James Dobson, and many other very gifted writers have had a major positive impact on my life and on my daily walk with the Lord. Elton Trueblood, the towering Quaker writer, has perhaps influenced me more than any writer outside the Bible. I am so thankful for and so appreciative of Christian writers and their ministry to me and my family. And I am smart enough to know that they would not be available to me without the dedicated Christian publishers and the outstanding Christian bookstores.

But we need to share the wealth. Why keep such good talent to ourselves? Why not let the rest of the world discover that Christian writing is just as good, just as helpful as the writing they find in their favorite bookstores? We need to use books to penetrate the world with positive alternatives. Whether through fiction or nonfiction, Christian writers need to be a part of the great literary mix that is so rich in this country.

The Christophers, whose motto "Better to light one candle than to curse the darkness" expresses a philosophy I admire, give annual awards for books, television specials, and motion pictures. These prestigious awards are for "writers, producers and directors who have achieved artistic excellence . . . affirming the highest values of the human spirit." In the most recent list of Christopher award winners, eleven books were cited. None of them, except a book for children entitled *Where Does God Live?* by a Jewish rabbi and a Catholic priest, have much of anything at all to do with a Christian message. None of the mainline Christian publishers were represented among award winners. I firmly believe that there were many books written by Christian authors and published by Christian publishers that "achieved artistic excellence and affirmed the highest values of the human spirit." I am just afraid that they have not been made available to the larger reading public. Even the Christophers don't know about them.

Of course, there are reasons why Christian writers are not represented in the secular market. Some of these reasons are legitimate. For example, most secular publishers will not accept a book that overtly extols the virtues of the Christian faith. To me, that's a serious flaw on their part, for they clearly aren't uneasy about promoting other "religions" such as the New Age and feminist witchcraft. But if this is a publishing fact of life, we need to find ways to get around it. Maybe it's not the best strategy to try write a book on evangelism and send it to a secular publisher. After all, these publishers are held accountable to the bottom line, and I think it's safe to say that the general reading public isn't interested in evangelism.

So the best way to get around the publishers' bias against overtly Christian books is to provide them with material they can sell. Here's where it gets tricky. For example, contemporary "thriller" novels are the current rage. Some are pretty trashy, but many are spellbinding page-turners that make for a good, entertaining read. Is there a way to "redeem" this genre for God? Personally, I believe that's what best-selling author John Grisham has done. Walk through any airport and you'll see several of his novels on the bookstore shelves. Or take a look at the *New York Times* best-seller list. As of this writing, two of his books were ranked numbers one and three. Not bad for a Southern Baptist layman from Mississippi.

Now if you pick up a copy of *A Time to Kill*, you may run across some rough language and rougher scenes. It's the story of a black man who avenged the rape of his young daughter. To me, the biblical theme of justice is effectively drawn out in such a way that any reader will walk away from that book with a renewed commitment to correcting wrong in this world. Had Grisham written a nonfiction book on the biblical concept of justice, it would never have been published by a secular publisher, let alone make the best-seller list. But by writing it as a novel and making it graphically realistic and accurate, he has become a roaring lamb.

Why couldn't some of our finest Christian authors do the same thing?

I believe many could, but it takes courage to break out of the ghetto. In the CBA universe a book might not sell very well, but an author very rarely gets figuratively pummeled and beaten about the head and shoulders by reviewers. It is rare to see a really negative review of a Christian book by Christian reviewers. Not so with books attempting to penetrate the broader market, the market where the salt of the Gospel is most needed. The standards are much higher and the scrutiny much more intense.

Chuck Swindoll in his classic message on the gospel of Luke, which calls all Christians to strive for excellence, has a special word for Christian writers. He says, "You never reach a place where you can be at ease with facts. Your task is to continually search, to study, to present the material in a careful and diligent manner. Get your facts straight. People are striving for a knowledge of the truth and you owe that to them. Be a wordsmith. Place value on communicating clearly and correctly and where you can, concisely. *If there is any place we can find shoddy and careless writing, alas, it is among the Christian ranks* (emphasis mine). Make a difference. Follow Luke's example."

Although Swindoll wasn't thinking of fiction writers, I think his advice applies here. To be a good fiction writer, you need to create realistic characters, situations, and scenes. Otherwise, your writing will be contrived, phony, sugar-coated. In fact, that's a pretty fair criticism of most Christian fiction and explains why very few novelists writing for Christians could get their books published by secular publishers. They are creating a false picture of the world. For any writer to make it into the secular market, he or she must be a wordsmith. Characters must be real people, with real problems and reactions. The settings must look like the world we all live in, and the plot must not appear to be manipulated by someone who wants everything to turn out okay. Real life doesn't happen that way.

One of the luxuries of writing to your own kind is that few Christian publications write the kinds of book reviews that appear in the secular press. We're generally pretty kind to Christian authors. But venture into the larger literary community, and you're liable to get skewered by nasty reviewers.

Consider what happened when Pat Robertson's book, *The New World Order,* began to attract attention outside the cozy world of Christian books. The *Wall Street Journal,* which is usually at least neutral regarding things Christian, carried a scathing review of the book. It was headlined "New World Order Nut." Here are some excerpts from that review:

"Pat Robertson is known to millions of Americans . . . as the host of the talk show, 'The Seven Hundred Club,' where his permanent village idiot's grin gives him the appearance of a trailer park David Letterman. . . . Having been rebuffed by the electorate, Mr. Robertson is now free to return to the space cadet political theories that got him off the ground in the first place. Those theories are contained in his new book, *The New World Order.* . . . In his energetically crackpot style, Mr. Robertson weaves a wild tale of international and extraterrestrial conspiracies, involving everyone from deposed Nicaraguan dictator Anastasio Somoza to Alger Hiss to Woodrow Wilson. . . . Still, as paranoid pinheads with a deep distrust of democracy go, he's a bit of a disappointment."

Then, Joe Queenan, the *Journal's* reviewer, ends his piece with a one word sentence: "Amateur."

Unfair? Unkind? Perhaps, but that's what you can expect when you publish a book in the larger secular publishing community. It's a lot safer submitting your book to the Christian community.

This gives us some idea of what the larger world is like for Christian writers and why it is so important that their books be meticulously researched, carefully written, scripturally sound, cogently reasoned, and intellectually credible if they hope to penetrate that world. We need to be out there, but only with our best. Even our best writing and best writers will be challenged and ridiculed. A clear presentation of the Gospel that shows the relevance of Christ to life in today's world will always meet resistance. Many will scoff, but, if it is our best work, some will be convinced, some will believe, some will be won. This is what being a roaring lamb is all about. It is not about an easy path. It is not about always winning. It is about being there, being where the battle is, where the salt is needed. As far as ridicule and persecution are concerned, when we begin to shy away from it and take the easy path, we need to reread Paul's description of his lot as he took salt to the ancient world. In 2 Corinthians 11:24–27 he says:

> Five times I received from the Jews the forty lashes minus one. Three times I was beaten with rods, once I was stoned, three times I was shipwrecked, I spent a night and a day in the open sea, I have been constantly on the move. I have been in danger from rivers, in danger from bandits, in danger from my own countrymen, in danger from Gentiles; in danger in the city, in danger in the country, in danger at sea; and in danger from false brothers. I have labored and

toiled and have often gone without sleep; I have known hunger and thirst and have often gone without food; I have been cold and naked.

Maybe Christian writers can stand a few tough reviews.

For those of you who think it's too much of a stretch to hope for Christian writers to enter the mainstream of secular publishing, consider the example of Phillip Johnson, the brilliant professor of law at the University of California at Berkeley. Professor Johnson, a person with impeccable academic credentials (he went to Harvard after his junior year in high school and then finished first in his law school class at the University of Chicago before being chosen clerk for U.S. Supreme Court Chief Justice Earl Warren), became convinced that the Darwinian theory of evolution was just that: a theory, unproved and unscientific, which took at least as much faith to believe as the story of creation as delineated in Genesis. The result of this conviction was a book that is one of the most important documents of the past several years. *Darwin on Trial* is a masterfully written, beautifully argued treatise that knocks a theory of creation without a Creator into the realm of the unbelievable.

Johnson knew that the easiest way to get *Darwin on Trial* published was to take it to a Christian publisher. He also knew that, strategically, that was the wrong place for it. He wanted a secular publisher to take the book to a secular readership. He wanted his book and his ideas to go head to head with those of the world; toe to toe with the Darwinists who insist that "man is the result of a purposeless and natural process that did not have him in mind," to use the words of Harvard paleontologist George Gayland Simpson.

Although he had a very difficult time finding a secular publisher willing to risk handling his book, once he did, Johnson's strategy worked brilliantly. His book was widely reviewed, became a topic of conversation in top academic circles, brought about many invitations to speak and debate on many college and university campuses and engendered many radio and television interviews. Johnson believes that little or none of this would have happened had he initially published via a Christian publisher, though he also believes he might have sold more books. Now that his book has been established, he is perfectly happy to have it marketed aggressively in Christian circles, and this is happening. This is a great example of a Christian writer thinking strategically and then courageously going with his best work out to do battle with the best the world has to throw at him.

I know there are many gifted thinkers and writers in the Christian community, and they are to be commended for sharing their knowledge with us through their books. But they also need to be writing for the larger public. They need to use their skills to become roaring lambs in the secular bookstore chains.

Another encouraging trend is the one in which a Christian publisher joins with a major secular publisher in copublishing certain books. This brings promotion and marketing to bear on both markets—the Christian Booksellers Association and the American Booksellers Association, the general audience bookstores. Thus, you will see a book such as Dave Dravecky's *Comeback* published by both Zondervan and Harper Collins. Let us hope that this trend will catch on and grow, helping to bring many more spiritually relevant books to an audience greatly in need of the message.

Being an entrepreneur myself, I am a strong believer in competition. I think even Christian publishing benefits from the strong competition among quality publishers. However, in the terribly difficult effort to reach the world with scriptural truth through the written word, some cooperative effort may be in order. I would like to see the Evangelical Christian Publishers Association truly live up to the "evangelical" part of their name and devise a cooperative strategy to help reach the wider world through books. Perhaps members of the ECPA could agree to join forces around even just one book a year, a book that would be chosen to be promoted, not in the Christian market but in the secular market. It would be an evangelical enterprise. An ECPA committee could be formed to select the association's yearly book to be taken to the secular market. Each member publisher could contribute to a marketing campaign that would fund advertising and an ambitious promotional tour by the writer. Monetary profits, if any, could be divided among the member publishers. Spiritual profits could be laid up as treasures in heaven. This may be a very naïve and impractical idea, but at least it is the kind of thinking that needs to be considered if we are to become the agents of change that we need to be.

What I am advocating is a radical change in our vision regarding the world of books. Currently, Christians write to each other, selling their books only in Christian bookstores. That's fine, but we need to press a little further. We need to see the bookshelves of Waldenbooks and B Dalton as the mission field. Our goal should not necessarily be to place books on evangelism or theology on those shelves, but to make sure great works of fiction and nonfiction written by our best Christian authors sit alongside the hundreds of titles that reach millions of readers. That's where we belong, and I believe it's possible for us to be there.

To do it, we need both more Christians who are writers and writers who are Christians. How do we get them? Again, the church needs to think strategically. When was the last time you heard a sermon encouraging young people to become writers? Local churches need to promote the idea that writing for the secular publishing world is a viable, yes Christian, ministry. Seminars and workshops need to be organized. The church library ought to contain books like Phillip Johnson's *Darwin on Trial* and Christopher DeVinck's *Power of the Powerless* and decent, well-written novels such as Anne Tyler's *Saint Maybe*. As Christians, we need to model good reading habits that include books from secular publishers so that our children will have a balanced view of reading and literature. If your church has even one young person who likes to write—whether it's poetry, short stories, science fiction, or whatever—that person ought to be nurtured and encouraged to use that interest for the Lord. Believe me, we will never see many roaring lambs in the writing profession if we don't start now to "grow our own."

Christian colleges and Christian publishers, particularly the Evangelical Christian Publishers Association, need to form a strong working alliance to see that the writing profession and writing ministry is supplied with the best possible talent in the future. The publishers need to be an active presence on Christian college campuses, meeting with faculty and students in mutually advantageous ways. Publishers need to show top Christian college students that writing is not only an important ministry but also a viable profession economically. I am afraid that gifted students are not shown how it is possible to make a living by writing. Obviously they do not have agents representing them, or contacts with publishers, or knowledge of the procedures involved in submitting and selling material. Through both campus seminars and workshops, as well as through internships at Christian publishing houses, publishing as a profession for Christians needs to be opened up to Christian students seeking ways to spend a productive professional life in ministry. It is certainly in the publisher's best interest to embark on such a program.

As people of the Book and believers in the Word, twentieth-century Christians must become widely known in publishing the truth. We must produce and distribute books that will help a needy world see and understand why Christ came, even if the great themes of the Gospel need to be lived out by characters in a superbly crafted novel. We must encourage our young people to pursue careers that will eventually get them writing articles for culture-shaping magazines like the *Atlantic, New Republic* (on whose staff, incidentally, Christian writer Fred Barnes is a senior writer), the *New Yorker*, and others. Established Christian writers need to devote at least a "tithe" of their time to writing for the secular world. Books of the highest possible quality written by skilled Christian authors who artfully weave biblical truth into their manuscripts must always be available to the people who need them most. They must never be out of print.

> "A little yeast works through the whole batch of dough."
>
> Galatians 5:9

The Visual Arts: A Cloudy
Lens, a Drab Palette

Prague is still a magnificent city. Beautiful old castles and soaring cathedrals in many ways make it the quintessential European city. When I saw Prague for the first time, I realized that this was the Europe I had envisioned as a child, long before my first trip to the continent. It is beautiful and very European, but forty years of repressive communist rule and misrule has robbed it of much of its color and practically all its gaiety. Now Prague and its people seem to exist only in various shades of grey.

During my visits to Prague, before the collapse of communism, there was a sinister feel to the place. Everyone was edgy and nervous, always looking over their shoulders. Taxi drivers often signaled for silence inside their cabs and asked you to step outside the cars for even the most innocuous of chats.

Once, after a few days of meetings with Czech television officials, I invited several of them to be my guests for a farewell lunch at a restaurant a few blocks from my downtown hotel. After dessert and coffee, I thanked them for their kindness to me during my stay and said I was going to walk back to my hotel and pack for my flight to Paris. My Czech friends became visibly nervous and asked me not to leave. I asked if they would like more coffee or more dessert. No, they wanted nothing more. Again, I moved to go. Again, they asked me to stay. I then asked if there was more business we needed to discuss before I left. No, they said, we had covered everything. Again, I moved to leave. Again, they almost begged me not to go. They were very nervous and embarrassed. Finally, the most senior of the gentlemen told me the reason they were keeping me in the restaurant. It seemed that while we were having lunch, there had been a shift change for the secret policemen assigned to follow me. The two who had, completely unbeknownst to me, followed me into the restaurant had left, but their replacements had not yet appeared. My friends felt there would be big trouble if I left the restaurant without my "tail."

We sat in a sort of strained silence for only a few more minutes before the senior official gave a pronounced affirmative nod that signaled everyone to get up and bid me a very cordial farewell. I walked back to my hotel trying to appear casual and at ease but probably looked both ridiculous and suspicious to the two plain-clothes policemen following me.

Only much later did I learn the reason for the significant official concern about a lone American moving alone around Prague. It seems the day I was to leave, a group of young Czech artists were to have an outdoor display of their work in one of the downtown squares. It was sure to be an explosive, confrontational situation. As it turned out, there was violence followed by arrests at the art exhibition. I was told that had I wandered off in the direction of the exhibit I would have been stopped and directed to return to my hotel. The request would have been made courteously at first but with as much force as necessary to keep me away from the exhibit.

A similar situation occurred on my first visit to Beijing. This was back in the seventies. The so-called Cultural Revolution had just ended, and I was the first American sports executive to enter a still-tense China since the normalization of relations with the U.S. Although the Chinese were anxious for me to come to help rebuild their shattered sports program, the conditions for my visit were very precise and very strict. I had to enter China alone—no entourage. Once I was there, where I stayed, whom I saw, and which cities I would visit would be strictly controlled by my Chinese hosts. No part of my schedule was provided for me in advance. And once I stepped aboard a Chinese government jet in Tokyo, I would be completely cut off from contact with anyone outside China until I was deposited in Hong Kong at the end of my visit. This was a little scary for this old Texan. However, the Chinese Olympic Committee, my official hosts, made me feel most welcome and I began to relax, go to work, and enjoy a great deal of wonderful Chinese food. (As guest of honor, at every meal, I did not enjoy the great "privilege" of eating the duck's brain, but I handled it by swallowing it whole like a pill.) My relationship with He Zhenliang, the head of the All China Sports Association and a fine gentleman, warmed rapidly. Before too many days, I felt at ease enough to ask Mr. He to take me to one place I particularly wanted to see. This was the Democracy Wall, which had received considerable coverage in the Western press. Here Chinese only recently freed from the terrible repression of the Cultural Revolution would come and paste hand-lettered posters espousing various political and social views. While this may not seem very exciting to Americans in the nineties, huge crowds would gather at the wall to read the posters and debate the messages. I wanted to see this firsthand and asked Mr. He to take me there. He agreed to drive me by in one of the few automobiles then in

Beijing but told me that we could not get out of the car and probably could not stop. The people at the wall were "too excitable," he said, and the presence of a Westerner might be "too provocative." Then Mr. He spontaneously made a most telling remark. He said, "I would not even dream of taking you to the area where the young artists are displaying their work. There the atmosphere is electric, explosive."

The incidents in Prague and Beijing underscore an important point. There is power in the visual arts, power to communicate important ideas, power to inspire, and power to inflame. It is no accident that totalitarian regimes have always moved quickly to control the visual arts. Painters, sculptors, photographers, and architects have always been quickly brought to heel when dictators have grabbed power. And, conversely, those artists who could and would convey the message of the tyrant(s) through their work became the darlings of the regime. It was the same in Nazi Germany and the Soviet Union as in Czechoslovakia and China. It is still the same in Castro's Cuba.

Christians seem to have forgotten the power of the visual arts. We are so verbal, so language-oriented that we have neglected painting, sculpture, photography, and architecture to the point where there is now almost no evidence of the gospel message, and no image of Christ in modern art. This is a tragedy, a disaster. Art has not lost its power because of our neglect. Its power is still there, but it is not being used for good. It is now most often used to advance the forces of evil, and, as always, the artists who are conveying the blasphemous, the profane, the nihilistic, and the sexually distorted messages are the darlings of the cultural elite in this and other Western countries. Satan is winning this battle.

The sorrow in this situation becomes more acute when we remember that down through the ages much of the greatest art and greatest architecture was created to glorify and exalt the Most High and His Son, Jesus Christ. The frustration becomes more acute when we realize that as those who are most closely in touch with the Creator we are demonstrating the least creativity. Christians with direct access to the Creator of the universe and with the indwelling of the Holy Spirit should be and could be the most brilliantly dazzling artists imaginable and should be and could be creating paintings, sculptures, photographs, and buildings that would draw men and women to the Savior and inspire them to great efforts in building God's kingdom. Please understand that I am not talking about the creation of idols and icons to be worshiped, but about great compelling works of art that would help to show the power and love of God in the world and in the lives of His children. Why isn't this happening? Why aren't Christians among the world's most noted artists? Why aren't Christians using God-given, finely honed, painstakingly developed artistic abilities to glorify God and inspire men and women to seek His highest for their lives? It is because, once again, we have fled the field, thrown in the towel, dropped out of the race. Again, we have abdicated, and for the most part the whole area of the visual arts has been left to those who do not care about God, about Christ.

My wife and I are very modest collectors of the works of a French painter by the name of Yolande Ardissone, who paints landscapes and seascapes in her native Brittany. We would like to be more than modest collectors but can afford only a small painting every few years. Ardissone is exclusively represented in America and in France by the Wally Findlay Galleries, large, well-known distributors, who handle many of the best-known American and international artists.

Several months ago I visited the Wally Findlay Gallery in New York. After establishing the fact that I was at least some sort of collector and at least superficially knowledgeable about one of the artists represented by the gallery, I asked the sales representative to show me what he had in Christian art. His response was, "Christian who?" He thought I had been asking to see works by a particular artist named Christian. I then explained that I was asking about art that had a religious or Christian theme or message. He looked puzzled, thought for awhile, and then said almost to himself, "I thought Christian art was an oxymoron. Aren't Christians against art?" Needless to say, he had no paintings to show me and seemed relieved when I said goodbye.

Now, I know there are talented Christians who paint, sculpt, and create artistic photographs. But their numbers are small. When is the last time your local art or photo gallery featured the work of a Christian artist or photographer and had the show reviewed by your newspaper's art critic?

You can go into almost any quality bookstore and get books of beautiful photographs on almost any subject you can name. But try asking for a book of photographs depicting the life of the church in America or featuring any area of the religious life of the nation. About the most you can hope for is a photo book on the Amish.

Quality art that depicts biblical themes is very hard to find. It is, however, easy to find works of art that glorify immoral behavior. Take, for example, the late Robert Mapplethorpe's widely acclaimed photographs of homosexuals engaged in sex acts. Or Andres Serranos's equally well-known photograph of the cross in a jar of urine. My hometown newspaper, the *Dallas Morning News*, recently covered a local art exhibit devoted exclusively to art using the cross as a theme. Here are some of the ways the cross was displayed in the exhibit as described by the newspaper: papered with dollar bills; covered with bingo cards and chips; shown with a Pee-wee Herman doll; covered with pennies;

burned, and the ashes put in a jar and framed. One piece "is a cross immersed in a jar of water that will be illuminated with a yellow lamp to tint the water. The jar also contains a plastic cheerleader whose outspread arms mimic the shape of the cross behind her. Confetti shaped like dollar signs and doves float in the water when the jar is shaken." Bob Sullivan, one of the gallery owners sponsoring the exhibit, said, "We did ask some artists—maybe this was wrong—to stay away from pornography per se. It's not only because it's controversial but because it seems so old hat." His wife said, "We want them [viewers] to see the humor in some of the work, to not take it too seriously." This kind of art and this kind of attitude is rather easy to find in any major city, but where are the contemporary exhibits depicting the Cross of Christ with reverence and power, illuminating the Savior and bringing home to viewers the real message of salvation? Hard to find.

The Christian community in America had for decades pretty much ignored the visual arts until recently when the art being purveyed across the land became so vile and so blasphemous that the church had to react. Because its own artistic strengths and abilities had been allowed to atrophy, sadly, once again the church could react only in a negative way. Once again the church was in no position to offer positive alternatives. It had none to offer. It could only cry out in anger and rage, evoking snickers from the cultural elite and ennui from the public at large.

Once again, the best we Christians could do was to call for boycotts, picketing, and demonstrations. Not surprisingly, Christian leaders such as Jerry Falwell and Donald Wildmon began raising money to fight this kind of art. They were particularly offended and incensed that tax dollars, via the National Endowment for the Arts, had helped to fund some of the most notorious works and their exhibition. This big tax-supported organization makes a great target, a great whipping boy. Maybe tax dollars should not be used to support art in this country, but making that the only battle cry of the church, the only organized expression of Christians about art in this country once again casts us in the role of censors and philistines. Once again, we are seen as only negative and reactionary. All that does is further alienate the serious artists who watch us whine and decide to have nothing to do with Christianity because it is, in their view, anti-art.

The chairman of the National Endowment for the Arts is appointed by and serves at the pleasure of the president of the United States. Our past three presidents—Jimmy Carter, Ronald Reagan, and George Bush—have, at the very least, been sensitive and sympathetic to the Christian church in America. Christians have had good access to the Oval Office and have, at the least, been heard on most issues. Why, then, do we have a National Endowment for the Arts that funds works so offensive to Christians and, really, to most decent Americans? I suspect it is because there has been no positive Christian initiative in this area. We have not put forward any Christians of stature knowledgeable in and articulate about the arts. Why? Because we don't know of any. Because we have not seen art as important. Because we have forgotten the power and the promise of the arts. Because we have abdicated. Because we only react.

How much better it would have been had we been able to respond to the Mapplethorpe and Serranos kind of garbage with positive alternatives. Instead of organizing boycotts, protests, and demonstrations, what if we had been able to mount competing exhibitions of great Christian paintings, sculpture and photographs in every city with Mapplethorpe and Serranos shows? What if every church in those cities announced a "Christian Arts Festival" to run during the duration of the exhibitions of filth?

Christian artists and their work could be honored. Children and the elderly could be bussed to see inspirational art. God, the Creator, could be glorified and His Son lifted up. Remember, the boycotts, protests, and demonstrations do nothing to tell who Christ is and nothing to proclaim His glorious truth. They provide no salt. Remember, our job as Christians is not primarily to protest, but to proclaim. To be roaring lambs for God. Paul said to the Colossians: "Naturally, we proclaim Christ. We warn everyone we meet, teach everyone we can, all that we know about Him so that we may present everyone at his full maturity in Christ" (1:28 PHILLIPS). Couldn't we do that with great, powerful images that depict God's grace? Is sin the only popular theme for artists?

Remember, too, that the National Endowment for the Arts is available to fund any artist who is enterprising enough to know how to write a grant proposal. I often wonder just how many Christian artists have submitted proposals. Here is a tool that the "other side" has learned to use to their advantage. Shouldn't we consider using this same tool rather than calling for it to be discarded?

As a Christian, I really do believe that "all things work together for good to those who love God." Therefore, when it comes to the fine visual arts of painting, sculpture, photography, and the like, I believe that kingdom-building good can come from the outrageous, blasphemous filth currently being purveyed as art. Good will come if the church is shocked into an understanding of how evil fills a vacuum when the people of God depart. Good will come if the church understands again the power and potential in art. If art can portray powerful messages of evil, it must also be used to convey even more powerful messages of hope, light, understanding, and grace. Good will come if the church and its people will begin to think both tactically and strategically about art and its role in building God's kingdom.

Certainly, if you believe the government is wrongfully using taxpayers' money to fund lousy art, it is your right and duty as an individual citizen to share your concern with the president and your congressmen and senators. But believe me, a brief personal letter from a constituent is far more powerful and persuasive to an elected official than having your name added to a list sent in by a lobbying group. In a recent such campaign Jerry Fallwell wrote, "I urge you to sign the enclosed petition to President Bush at the bottom of this page and return it with your emergency gift to Liberty Alliance today. . . . We will tally the returns and send them to the President." Evidently the "emergency gifts" will be used to pay for tallying the returns and paying for the postage to send them on to the president. Let's bypass the middleman, save God's money, and communicate directly and individually to our own representatives. It will be more effective, and we can use the "emergency gift" money to help tell who Christ is and why He came.

I need to say here that I admire Jerry Falwell and much of what he does. I recently spoke on the campus of his Liberty University and was thrilled to see the beautiful campus and to meet so many of the wonderful students deeply committed to Christ and His service. I only wish that Falwell, Wildmon, and other powerful Christian leaders would lead us toward positive Christ-revealing responses to problems facing our nation. I wish they would help us to proclaim Him as the answer to every problem we face, including the problem of art devoid of God.

For example, what if the communication I received from Jerry Falwell had said, "Urgent. . . . Urgent. . . . Urgent. . . . Urgent. Action needed immediately!" (as his recent communication began) and had then gone on to say, "The situation with the visual arts in this country has gotten so bad and is so bereft of any Christian influence that the church must act and act now. We are convening, here on the campus of Liberty University, an emergency meeting of Christian leaders, artists, and those interested in the arts to discuss ways our families, churches, and colleges can begin to retake the lost territory in the arts for Christ and His cause. The church of Jesus Christ needs to address the problem head on in positive and productive ways. Please send a small donation to help us fund this much-needed Christian strategy session." If I had received that kind of message from Falwell, I would have been a player. I would have made a contribution. I might even have tried to wangle an invitation to the conference.

Here is an example of another kind of appeal that would have brought a positive response from me: "Here at Liberty University we are trying very hard, under the leadership of the Holy Spirit, to build an art department that will be at least the equal of any in the country. Why are we doing this? We want to train young Christian men and women of talent to use their God-given skills in the visual arts in ways that will glorify Christ. The church needs painters, sculptors, and photographers to help tell the salvation story and to provide positive, alternative art to blunt the attack of artists working only for evil. Please help us."

Another example of the kind of appeal I would support: "Here at Liberty University we are praising God for the many talented young people He has led to our campus. Let me tell you about just one of them and ask for your help. Joe Jones is an amazingly talented photographer. We think he has the potential to be a Christian Ansel Adams and to bless the world with his work. His desire is to serve God with his photographic abilities. We need some special one-time gifts to get for Joe both some specialized equipment he needs and some advanced training not available here at Liberty. Please help us to equip and train this young man who is going out as a missionary to serve God with his camera."

I think you get the idea. We have a tremendous network of people who are usually called upon to donate to campaigns based on fear, campaigns that are defensive in their entire approach. It's time to go on the offensive—to unleash this army of supporters in creative campaigns that produce something good to plug into the mainstream of American culture. In my circles, Christians are thought of as people who are against things. I want us to be known as people who are *for* things good, wholesome, creative, wonderful, and fulfilling. That's the message of the Gospel and it ought to be the message in all that we do.

So how do we begin to reclaim the visual arts? How do we become roaring lambs in this important area of life? As with so many things, we must begin with the family. Christian mothers and fathers need to begin to appreciate the importance of the arts. We need to become informed about them and to pass the information on to our children. We also need to surround ourselves and our children with examples of good art. I believe every home should have at least one original painting, drawing, sculpture, or photograph displayed, even if it's a watercolor your third-grader made in school. Frame it, mount it on a wall, and make a big deal about it. If you can't afford to buy other works of art, acquire books or prints. Most of all, if any of your children show a special interest in the arts, encourage them. Explain to them that this is a gift from God and can be used to His glory.

I am constantly amazed at how parents will encourage their children to pursue musical talents but not visually artistic talents. Maybe this helps explain why there are so few Christians in the visual arts. As parents, we can change that. It is important to teach that an interest in art does not somehow make a person less manly or womanly. Attack the myth that somehow the greatest creativity is reserved for heathens; that to be an artist one must push not only the limits of taste but of personal behavior and lifestyle as well. This is a lie, a lie from Satan. God, the Creator, gives good gifts to His children, and these include creativity, inspiration, and talent.

Churches also need to be involved in a positive way with the arts. Christian artists need to be supported. Where possible, use their work in decorating the church. Perhaps some churches could become "patrons" of promising Christian artists. Your church could also sponsor special Christian art events, such as having an annual exhibit or inviting a Christian artist to speak about the way God speaks through art. Most of all, every church should encourage its young people to see art as a possible means of serving both God and man. Demonstrate appreciation for beautiful, compelling, inspirational works of art.

By the way, the church building itself ought to reflect the beauty and creativity of our Lord. Perhaps in a misunderstanding of stewardship and piety, most evangelical churches have selected a rather bland and uninteresting style of architecture. If your church is planning to build, at least consider designs that may be a little bit out of the ordinary. In addition to your necessary emphases on function and effeciency, place some emphasis on worship, on the image you will leave on your community. Even simple, cost-effective designs can be a work of art. Remember, we've given the impression to the rest of the world that Christians are opposed to art. Why not respond with a church building that uplifts even the casual passerby?

Of course, your church may be a long way off from building a new facility. Can your present facility be "upgraded" so that it is viewed as an asset to your community? Little things like professional landscaping, a new coat of paint, perhaps removing the '50s-style steeple and replacing it with something more contemporary go a long way toward showing the community that Christians do indeed appreciate and support beauty. Inside, consider acquiring and displaying original paintings or sculpture. Again, these do not have to be expensive, but they make a strong statement about your church's appreciation of art.

Incidentally, although Christians in the arts are presently a minority, they are not entirely absent. Photographers like Eileen Pope of Miami and painters like Ed Knippers of Washington D.C., as well as a loose-knit group of artists who belong to the group, Christians in the Visual Arts (CIVA, Box 10247, Arlington, VA 22210), the roaring lambs of the art world. But clearly, the need is great for more fine Christian artists out there on the cutting edge of creativity.

Finally, Christian colleges and universities need to become actively, robustly involved in reclaiming the visual arts for the kingdom. If you are an alumnus, a trustee, or supporter of a Christian college, encourage its administration to give special attention to its art department in these critical days. My knowledge of art departments in Christian colleges is certainly not very broad. From my limited observation, however, I would say that at most Christian colleges, art is a sort of academic afterthought. Not much time, attention, or money are devoted to it. The department is usually tucked away in an abandoned building where the students and faculty are ignored. No one is articulating very clearly, or at least very loudly, how the fine-arts program fits into the overall educational and spiritual goals of the Christian college. The results—the paintings and sculpture—for the most part, reflect this neglect. To put it more positively, where the administration and the entire college community have a clear understanding of the relationship between art and faith, students and faculty in the art department create stunning art. There's no reason why our Christian colleges cannot "feed" decent, remarkable art into the cultural mainstream.

Christians need to reclaim the galleries and exhibits for the kingdom of God. Not in a triumphalistic, competitive manner, but as generous contributors of the talents God gives them. We need to show the world in powerful, positive ways that artists devoted to God and to building His kingdom do not work with a cloudy lens or a drab palette, but, on the contrary, they see the world more clearly and colorfully because of His power in their lives.

Do not conform any longer to the pattern of this world, but be transformed by the renewing of your mind.

Romans 12:2

8

The Christian Academe: Underachievers

Neither guinea nor pig. That is how some cynics see the Christian college. In the same way that a guinea pig is neither a guinea nor a pig, they will say, the Christian college is, in many cases, neither Christian nor a college. This may be true in some cases, but I am thankful that in most it is not. I know of many institutions of higher education in America that are both Christian, in that they openly honor and serve Christ, and colleges, in that they are communities of learners, actively seeking and teaching truth. In fact, there are up to eighty fully accredited American colleges where Jesus Christ is at the center of all that is done. These institutions are a tremendous potential resource for the church in America.

Are they fulfilling their mission? No way. If they were, the preceding chapters, and indeed this entire book, would be largely unnecessary. Christian colleges have great potential for good and for kingdom building. They are, for the most part, underappreciated, underutilized, underfinanced, and underproductive. As good as they are, they are not making as great a contribution as they could be making. If the lambs are going to roar in America, Christian colleges must become more intentional about training a generation of culture shapers.

I write about Christian colleges as one who loves them. I first set foot on a Christian college campus as a student in the fall of 1951. From that day to this, I have had a love affair with Christian higher education in America. For more than forty years, I have been involved as a student, an athlete, a teacher, a coach, an administrator, a trustee, and an active alumnus with Christian colleges. In all, I have been closely associated with five different institutions and have had more than a passing acquaintance with dozens of others. I met my wife at a Christian college. Both of our daughters graduated from that same institution. I currently sit on the boards of two Christian colleges. While I certainly do not have all the answers or perfect insight where America's Christian colleges are concerned, I feel reasonably qualified to pass along some thoughts for consideration. I offer them in the conviction that "he has the right to criticize who has the heart to help."

Think with me for a moment about the absolutely tremendous resource the Christian colleges are for the church in America. Each truly Christian college is there for the avowed purpose of educating students for effective Christian living. In the best cases, every faculty member shares that purpose. Well-qualified young people go to these campuses, mostly because they want to be there. Someone is paying a premium for them to attend. For nine months a year, for a four-year period, at a time when they are most pliant, most teachable, they are a captive audience. In the classrooms, in the dorms, in a chapel, in church, with counselors, on the athletic fields, on dates (well, perhaps not on all dates), and in the library they are subjected to Christian ideas and ideals. After four very expensive years in this wonderful environment, many should emerge as roaring lambs penetrating American society in all legitimate fields, rising to the top because of merit and character, and winsomely communicating the Gospel through their work.

In reality, few roaring lambs are coming from our Christian colleges.

Christian college graduates typically have commitment, but not confidence. They have ideals, but not vision. Except for those going into the professional ministry, no one has laid out for most of them either the possibilities or the responsibilities of penetrating every area of our society with the message of Christ. The four-year investment is not paying nearly the kingdom dividends it should.

Why aren't these wonderful institutions with well-trained, dedicated faculties producing the roaring lambs the times demand? It is because we both give them too little and ask too little of them.

The church in America has never given its colleges the financial support they need and deserve. Most Christian colleges operate under severe budget restrictions that ultimately affect the self-image of everyone connected with the school. The temptation for many is to think of the Christian college as second-rate, which simply is not true. But if our young people and their faculty are constantly reminded that giving is down, budgets are being cut, and services are being curtailed, how can we expect lions to come roaring out of the Christian college? Both individual churches and affiliated denominations will do well to reconsider their support of Christian higher education. The schools need and deserve more, much more.

I would love to see every church in America "adopt" at least one Christian college. In the same way that a church chooses to support missionaries in whose ministry they believe, churches should select a Christian college whose theology and mission statement is compatible with its own and then support it with regularly budgeted gifts. I'm not talking about an occasional offering but a regular item in the general church budget to make sure the giving is consistent. Along with financial support should come copious amounts of prayer. And certainly the young people of the church should be encouraged to consider attending this "adopted" Christian college.

In the lore of every Christian college there are stories of families who have made extraordinary sacrifices for their sons and daughters to be able to attend. Unfortunately, that kind of zeal and that kind of concern seem to be largely in the past. Now, too often, even Christian families base too much of their decision about their children's higher education on cost alone. A Christian college education will almost invariably cost more than a community- or state-supported education. Yet the differences in price will be small in the light of eternal considerations.

Should every Christian family automatically send their children to a Christian college? Absolutely not! For one thing, the secular schools need some roaring lambs on their campuses, too. Deeply committed Christian young people need to take their faith and values onto the university campus. But Christian parents ought to at least consider a Christian college education for their sons or daughters, and the question of cost should not be the only deciding factor. Many young people need the Christian nurture as well as the integration of faith and learning that come with a Christian college education. Also, in a smaller setting, young people with unpolished skills and talents will be nurtured in ways that are not possible on a larger campus. Some parents encourage their children to attend a Christian college primarily to increase the chances that they will find a Christian mate. Don't laugh!

Considering the condition of marriage today, if all your son or daughter got out of a Christian college education was a wonderful Christian spouse, it would still be quite a bargain.

After that nice little commercial for Christian colleges, let me address a few words to my colleagues in Christian higher education. As we increase our support and sacrifice to send you our children, we will also increase our expectations. All too often, everyone in Christian higher education—faculty, administration, parents, students—expect less than the best when the label "Christian" is applied. That has to change. Administrators have to provide the same level of leadership competence that one would expect to find at Harvard. Faculty members need to continually upgrade themselves both in content and method. Students need to hold to rigorous standards of scholarship, with learning taking precedence over ministry. And parents need to stand behind the school's effort to produce leaders.

A Christian college faculty member recalled an experience with a student I'll call Sandy. She entered her freshman year on academic probation, meaning she had not met the minimal standards for admission to the school and had to toe the mark by the end of the first semester. Within two weeks my friend noticed her work was slipping, so he asked to speak with her privately. When he mentioned the quality of her work and asked if she was having problems adjusting to college, she replied, "Oh no, college is great. I love it here. But I'm having trouble finding time to study. I have a morning prayer group before breakfast, then a Bible study after supper, and I've joined a ministry team that works with kids downtown."

Poor Sandy thought a Christian college was youth camp with a few classes on the side. Her parents were thrilled to get reports of all this spiritual activity, and even my professor friend was reluctant to squelch her spiritual development. But he swallowed hard and said, "God sent you here to develop your mind so you can serve Him better. Drop out of all your Bible studies and ministry teams, skip vespers if you have to, but start studying."

We need to expect our Christian colleges to be just as tough as any other private school or university. Unless we demand excellence at our Christian colleges, we will continue to produce too many graduates who are content to sit on the sidelines and let the "big-name Christians" try to change the world. As I've already shown (and you already know), that isn't working. We need roaring lambs who will turn this nation back toward its Judeo-Christian foundation.

I'm afraid too many of our Christian colleges have developed an inferiority complex. Obviously, relatively small Christian colleges cannot compete with giant research institutions in terms of facilities and equipment. There will probably never be any atom smashers or giant radio telescopes on Christian college campuses. So what? Undergraduate education—even in the sciences—does not demand expensive, sophisticated equipment. Basic laboratory equipment and solid, godly science teachers who demand excellence will give our students the knowledge and skills necessary to get them into medical schools and into graduate programs at the universities. More and more employers are looking for graduates from liberal arts colleges—graduates who have been well schooled in the world of books, words, ideas, ideals, history, ethics, speech, communication, and creativity. No expensive equipment is needed here. For the most part, we already have the most important "equipment" in the form of well-trained, highly motivated, dedicated faculties. We need to pay them better, encourage them to reach higher in their own scholarship, and expect them to set examples of excellence for our students, while accepting nothing but excellence from them. In many cases, our faculties, like our students, are not being adequately challenged.

There are some who would have us believe that tough, demanding teachers and an uncompromising commitment to excellence are not compatible with the concept of a loving, caring, redemptive community, which we also expect a Christian college to be. This is an example of the kind of flabby thinking that keeps Christians from being optimally prepared to meet the challenges of representing Christ effectively in an alien environment. This is the kind of thinking that makes excuses. Nowhere in Scripture, in the Old or New Testament, do we see God calling us to be anything but our best. Certainly our colleges—which are also His colleges—should operate on the same principle.

Because the overall direction and philosophy of the Christian college comes from the executive leadership and board of trustees, special attention must be given to the way these positions are filled. Sometimes, the president of a college is allowed to continue serving despite obvious deficiencies simply because the trustees have not stepped up to their responsibility to hold the president accountable. And why should they? In most cases, the president and his top administrators have a strong role in selecting new board members, and the temptation exists for some administrations to build a board that comes to meetings, has a good time, and asks no tough questions. In the worst of situations, boards of Christian colleges can become "good old boy" clubs. There's too much at stake for this attitude and practice to creep into Christian colleges, but I have seen it happen. If you are an alumnus of or regular contributor to a Christian college, speak up if you sense this is happening at your school. Excellence will never characterize a Christian college if the highest level of leadership—the president and the board of trustees—does not operate with integrity and professionalism.

This commitment to excellence is needed for many reasons. Among the most important is the need to combat the debilitating inferiority complexes with which the majority of Christian college graduates are burdened. Too often they feel that as graduates of a small Christian college, they are not adequate to go head to head with the world in important arenas of ministry. Too often they are not challenged to think beyond certain professions and certain levels in those professions. Certainly a first-grade teacher can be just as important to God and His kingdom as a secretary of state. A writer of Sunday school literature can accomplish as much for God as a syndicated columnist whose work appears in *The New York Times*. This is not about developing a hierarchy of service. It is about Christians being able to penetrate every area of our world and being able to fill the role God may prescribe for them. If we are not preparing the next governor, novelist, TV anchor, or filmmaker, we can never expect to find a Christian influence in those culture-shaping professions. If those who have a role in Christian higher education would make an uncompromising commitment to excellence with faith that God will help them achieve it, we could see amazing things happen in the lives on our graduates. We would see some real roaring lambs go out from our colleges to make the right kind of noise in the right kind of place.

Another important reason we need this commitment to excellence was articulated so well by C. S. Lewis when he wrote,

> If all the world were Christian, it might not matter if all the world were uneducated, but as it is, a cultural life will exist outside the church, whether it exists inside or not. To be ignorant and simple now, not be able to meet the enemies on their own ground, would be to throw down our weapons and to betray our uneducated brethren who have, under God, no defense but us against the intellectual attacks of the heathen. Good philosophy must exist, if for no other reason, because bad philosophy needs to be answered.

So much "bad philosophy" is being foisted upon society, and we betray our "uneducated brethren," who have "no defense but us" every time we allow significant error to be portrayed as fact without a scripturally based rebuttal.

Many of our best Christian colleges are either into or approaching their second century of service. They are a tremendous God-given resource. They have been preserved to this day through enormous effort, great sacrificial giving, much prayer, and God's grace. With all the good they do, all the lives they impact for good, and all the positive influence they are on society, much of their potential for the building of God's kingdom is untapped and unrealized. Both churches and individual Christians must become better informed about our Christian colleges. Better, more productive connections must be formed. More strategic investments of the church's resources must be made in the schools. Christian parents and Christian students should prayerfully consider a Christian college education. Many more of the church's strongest, most able, most astute members must make themselves available and must be recruited for quality service on the trustee boards of Christian colleges.

Most of all, everyone associated with Christian colleges—students, faculty, administrators, trustees, alumni, individual donors, constituent churches—should expect and demand that every Christian college be committed to a standard of excellence so that the world will get a clearer picture of the ultimate excellence of our Lord Jesus Christ.

We cannot afford underachievers in the Christian academe.

Fight the good fight of the faith.

1 Timothy 6:12

9

A Final Word: Getting It Done

In the preface I wrote that this book would be more about opportunities missed than opportunities taken. Since writing those words, I have thought a lot about why this has been true. Why have I not roared more? I believe the primary reasons are a lack of awareness and a lack of understanding. Not too original, but all too true.

Far too often, when I was in the midst of an opportunity to say something, write something, or do something that would have been a positive response to Christ's command to be salt, I was not aware of it. I was not alert. For far too long I did not understand what my responsibilities and privileges were. No one had impressed on me the obligation I had as a Christian to obey the Scriptures in this area of my life, nor had I been made to understand the joy that obedience brings. I was not smart enough to pick it up on my own. Even after reading Trueblood's great book *The Company of the Committed*, even after memorizing and being sort of haunted by its statement that "the test of the vitality of a religion is to be seen in its effect upon culture," I still did not become involved and productively engaged. I missed many opportunities and many chances for the quiet exhilaration of fulfillment that comes when people know that to the very best of their ability they are doing what they can do to advance God's kingdom. I do not want the readers of this book to miss that.

The happy reality is that no one needs to miss it. Christ commanded each one of us to be salt. Both His love for us and His perfection would not allow Him to command what we cannot fulfill. Each of us can get it done. We can all make it happen.

Even with all my missed chances, God has continued to give me opportunities. Let me share one with you. He led the great major league pitcher Dave Dravecky across my path. Dave, long committed to Christ, was about to lose his pitching arm to cancer. He was not about to lose something much more important to him—his wonderful effectiveness as a witness to Christ's supreme place in his life.

With the help of talented Christian writer Tim Stafford (another Roaring Lambs Hall of Famer), Dave had just written a dramatic story of his life in baseball and his life of faith even in the face of cancer. The book, *Comeback*, had reached and is reaching many. Now it seemed that a television/video documentary on his life could be the next tool that God would have Dave use in his ministry of witness. God gave Dave and me an identical vision for what the documentary should be. His sparkling wife, Jan, who is a full partner in all Dave does, shared the vision. With great effort and the effective help of many talented people, we produced the one-hour documentary, "Dravecky: A Story of Courage and Grace."

From the very beginning there were those who wanted to dilute the part that God and faith played in Dave's story. From the very beginning Dave said no. First of all, they didn't want the word "grace" in the title—too religious. Next, we were told there

was too much "God talk" in the script. They wanted more baseball and less religion. We said no. We compromised where we
could, but kept in the essential elements of Dave's conversion and
commitment.

At the premiere, we faced a sort of quintessential moment of
truth. The first audience to see the production was one made up of
very sophisticated New Yorkers. They had paid one hundred dollars
apiece to attend the opening as a benefit for the Memorial Sloan-
Kettering Cancer Research Center. As the program was projected on
the big screen for this audience made up of major league baseball
executives, some of our country's top medical experts, wealthy
donors to cancer research, and a scattering of New York's notably
cynical sports writers, it was nail-biting time. Would this tough audience sit still for, accept, and appreciate a clear presentation of the
Gospel and a life of faith as told by Dave and Jan Dravecky?

As the program closed and the last strains of "Prayer" by Petra
faded away, there was a brief moment of silence, the ultimate
pregnant pause. Then, thunderous (at least to my ears) applause
began. Dave walked to the front of the theater, and the audience,
still applauding, rose to their feet. I was in the back of the theater,
but as the applause swept over Dave, our eyes met, and in a ges-
ture of exhilaration, I sort of threw my fist in the air as a salute to
Dave and as an expression of thanksgiving. In spite of my past failures and omissions, in spite of many opportunities I had missed,
in spite of my slowness to understand, God had presented an
opportunity and had helped me not to blow it. The lambs roared.
It was wonderful. It was humbling.

The reason to include the Dravecky story here is not to say
that for you to be really effective it is necessary for a great major
league baseball player with a dynamic testimony to be brought
into your life. That is certainly *not* the point. The point is that no

matter how late it is in your Christian life, no matter how little you have been involved, no matter how many opportunities you have missed, God will continue to make it possible for you to do meaningful things. Stay awake. Stay alert.

A much more important point is that there is literally unlimited opportunity for every Christian—every man, woman, and child—to be fully involved, totally engaged every day in obeying the scriptural admonition to be a preserving salty influence in society. And the point is that your *positive* involvement will produce many positive results in your own life and in the lives of many others. Perhaps the most exciting, life-enriching benefit will be a sense of fully participating in kingdom building. You can *do* Christianity as well as *be* a Christian.

Some time ago my friend Bill Bullard, who has a wonderful and unique ministry to upscale business men and civic leaders, told me that one of the biggest problems Christians and the Christian church faced was finding a place for everyone to "take hold." New Christians almost intuitively want to serve, want to be energetically and productively involved in the life of faith, but they don't know how to start or where to begin. And no one seems to be able to tell them. In church, some can teach Sunday school, some can be in the music program, some can work with youth, but there are only so many jobs there. What are the great mass of the other people to *do?* Are the rest of us to be only spectators at performances and auditors of information? Many are trapped in this kind of Christian torpor and, after an initial burst of zeal, become sadly resigned to only occupying a pew and contributing financially to the work of others. But if we really understand both the necessity and the possibility of being salt and being really alert, we will see that we can all be everyday front-line Christians, and we will see many places to take hold.

One way in which everyone can be a player and be a leader is in helping raise people's level of alertness. Ministries need to be asking their elder boards and their congregations, "What active positive strategy does this church have regarding Christ's command to be salt? How are we marshaling and deploying our forces and our resources to be engaged in our community in such a way that the spread of evil and error is retarded? How can we play our part in making the community we live in a better, more productive place, and how can we give it a longer-lasting vision for effective evangelism? What kind of God-glorifying alternatives can we provide for those things that are antithetical to building His kingdom?

If your pastor and/or your board of elders is not asking those questions of you, *you* should be asking those questions of *them*. Raise their level of awareness. Keep them alert. Get them in gear.

Someone needs to be asking the same questions in every Sunday school class and every Bible-study group and needs to keep asking them until there is a plan and a strategy for engagement. And remember, an effective strategy doesn't end with just recounting the evil. Just telling each other how terrible television is or how awful the movies are or how shameful it is that the local school board is planning for condom distribution in city schools is not a strategy. It does not produce a plan of action. Just bewailing the fact that the editorial page of your local paper only rarely carries a William Murchison or a Cal Thomas column doesn't really help. An effective strategy calls for positive action. The answer is not in canceling your subscription to the paper. It is in determining that someone should write a letter of thanks to the publisher every time a Murchison or Thomas column does appear. Or assigning someone to write a letter extolling the virtues of these columns and asking that they be considered for regular inclusion.

A "roaring lamb" solution to the problem of a godless school board policy comes in coalescing around a Christian candidate in the next school board election (or becoming such a candidate) or in articulating in a cogent, practical, good-spirited letter to the editor a scripturally based suggestion for change. All too often Christians, when they have become involved in these highly emotional situations, are seen as red-faced ranters and ravers, with neck veins popping and placards waving in protest. We need a strategy of proclamation, not protest. We need to be positive, not negative, and we need to present alternatives—a better way.

My point is that we really *can* do something about the condition our world is in. The same questions that we need to ask of our church leaders and of our Sunday school classes and growth groups need to be asked of our families and, finally and most importantly, they need to be asked of ourselves. Even if we are rebuffed by our pastor and cannot interest our Christian friends or families, we can engender a productive alertness within ourselves. We can recognize both our responsibilities and our opportunities and can *act* accordingly. Then, when those around us see our effort and our joy, many will, I believe, want to join in.

At the most basic level, regardless of what our gift or gifts might be, we can all support good and godly projects and enterprises and avoid those that are evil. If every Christian would do only these two things in a very positive way, our society and our world would be dramatically affected for good. A powerful salty solution would penetrate, and the roar of many lambs would create the sweetest music this side of heaven. If on the rare occasion when something really good is on television every Christian would first watch and would then write a letter of appreciation to the network and sponsors, what do you think would happen? If, when the worst of television is airing, tens of millions of Christians would refuse to watch, what do you think would happen? There would be no need for boycotts or petitions or hand wringing. Television would almost immediately begin to change for the better. The sad and sobering truth is that American Christians support much of the worst of the popular television programs. Without this support, the networks and advertisers would change the programming.

Regardless of what others may or may not do, each one of us can, at the very least, begin a life of active, effective ministry to our community by simply supporting good projects, programs, and events and avoiding the bad ones. It does not take special talent or a special gift to just say thanks when someone or some organization does something that honors God and His Word. Stay awake. Stay alert. Say thanks. Support the good and refuse to support the bad. Doing this will provide a foundation of ministry for every Christian. Everyone can begin to be involved. Everyone can make a positive contribution.

Supporting good things and eschewing the bad provides a starting point for all. However, many will want and need to go far beyond this minimal but effective service. Perhaps many will begin to see that they have talents and gifts that both allow and require them to do more. Many should become involved locally. Some should work in a national arena. There is a place for all. Let us hope that all will also remember that roaring in the most effective way requires involvement, penetration, and the supplying of positive alternatives—alternatives that point people to God's Son. Don't get bogged down in the negatives, in protests, and boycotts. Spend your time and money in ways that will help proclaim the truth of God.

Sure, there will be times when we need to take a stand *against* evil as well as doing something positive to replace it. But we need to choose our battles more wisely and fight with dignity and a winsome spirit. Jana Spencer, the wife of one of my colleagues, can get a hearing for her concern about the books in the library of her son's school because she has baked tens of dozens of cookies for years of PTA functions and has helped decorate the gym for every pageant in memory. But when she actually decided to do something, she didn't rant and rave and make harsh demands. Instead, she marshaled her facts, had meetings with the librarians and the PTA, and succedeed in making sure that her sons wouldn't be subjected to literature promoting evil. Her lamb's roar counts and is heard because she has won a hearing. (I'd put her in my Roaring Lambs Hall of Fame if she'd just go back and identify quality childrens books that *should* be in school libraries and then help the school find funds to purchase them.)

The good news, then, is that every Christian can be a roaring lamb. It is not necessary to wait for anyone to begin. We can all begin to raise awareness levels, particularly our own. We can all, at the very least, begin to support good, godly efforts and avoid bad, ungodly ones. We can all assess our individual talents and abilities and begin to use those in the most appropriate ways. It may be in writing a letter to the local paper or an essay in *Newsweek*. It may be in organizing an exhibition of the work of Christian photographers or in taking and developing our own God-glorifying photographs. It may be in helping a Christian college to attain excellence or in helping a young person attend such a college. We can all begin. Now.

As effective as individual Christians can be—and with God's help one person acting alone can do mighty things—it is almost always true that acting in concert we can do even more. When the body of Christ works in harmony and unison, the most effective kingdom building is done. Although we should not wait to begin our own individual ministries of penetration, involvement, and positive alternatives, our goal should always be to energize the church toward a corporate strategy. We should never use our pastor's apathy or a lack of interest on the part of our fellow church members as an excuse for our lack of action, but our constant goal should be to marshall the largest, most effective force possible. For most of us that force is our local church. When a church really roars, the world really hears.

To inspire you to work toward being in such a church, let me describe for you my vision of a church full of roaring lambs: This church would have an awareness of its obligation to fulfill Christ's command to be salt and would make that command the priority it deserves to be. It would understand the possibility of involving every member. This awareness and understanding would be played out in many ways in the life of the church.

In this church, there would be a "roaring lambs committee," a board or commission with standing equivalent to a missions committee. (It is important to note that being salt is *not* evangelizing per se. It is an important adjunct to evangelism but is a response to a separate and distinct command warranting its own special emphasis and attention.) As planning for the work of this church takes place, there should be a plan and strategy for making the church as effective as possible in this important endeavor.

When the pastor would map out his curricular approach to his teaching for the year, he would be sure that there would be a series of sermons on salt, just as there is on evangelism and missions. And he would attempt to explain how to shake the salt effectively on areas of need, emphasizing the church's commitment in each area and the opportunity for all to be involved.

If the church is a small one, the roaring-lambs committee might decide on an area of specialization. It may be that essentially all the energies of the church in this regard will involve supplying quality books to the libraries of local schools. It may be that this particular church has a few talented writers, who, working together, can craft important letters to the editor of the local newspaper or develop guest columns or op-ed pieces. All members of the small congregation can offer suggestions for topics that need to be addressed and give helpful critiques of the writers' efforts.

The roaring-lambs committee in a large church should be encouraging and organizing activities and action across a broad spectrum of interests. There should be a committee to acquire art for the church, to display the work of Christian artists, and to encourage the art of its own members. Christian writers should be brought in for workshops. Christian publishers should be visiting to discuss writing as a career with the young people of the church.

A committee should be assigned to build a solid relationship with key writers and editors of the local newspapers. The staff at the paper should know what church member (a lay person) to call when a quote is needed in the area of religion or when a biblical question needs answering. The editors should know that they can count on solid, compelling guest columns to run in important holiday editions. They should also know that the writers of the church are prepared to develop columns on controversial topics from a biblical perspective. The way to be most effective with your local newspaper is to first develop relationships. Don't just start sending material in "over the transom." Meet with key editors, columnists, and writers. Spring for lunch. Let them see that you are there to serve them as well as your church and the kingdom.

The same kind of strategy should be used with radio and television, especially with the producers and hosts of increasingly popular talk shows. Obviously, anyone representing the church on a live broadcast, which can often be confrontational, must be well prepared and unfailingly polite and good natured while still making points for truth. This person should also be supported by the prayer of the congregation. We do need to be out there with our most skilled people.

The movie subcommittee of the church's roaring lambs committee should be doing everything from planning film festivals made up of "Films of the Faith" to organizing mass attendance at films of Christian producers that come to town.

One group of church members should be assigned to develop, maintain, and exploit (in the best sense of that word) a relationship with a selected Christian college. Perhaps someone from the church should be on the college board. Choirs and other musical groups from the college should be scheduled to perform. Visits to campus should be organized for the young people of the church. The college should be held accountable for the funds the church donates to it and should be encouraged to strive for excellence.

These are only a few examples of how a church that really takes seriously the necessity for positive involvement with its community can begin to be involved and can provide a way for every member to take part.

An important overlay for all the activities of every church, large and small, needs to be a constant, ongoing, very serious effort to make sure that young people increasingly see every career and every occupation as a ministry. There should be no less support or attention for an earnest Christian young person who has been accepted to the Julliard School of Music than for one going off to seminary. The church needs writers, performers, artists, speakers, politicians, businessmen, and workers in every craft and trade. In God's eyes there is no hierarchy. There certainly should not be in ours.

Regarding our young people, let me address a special concern that may have kept us from sending our children off to careers in theater, television, film, the arts, journalism, etc. These fields have a fairly well-deserved reputation for being especially hazardous in terms of lifestyle and personal behavior. I'm painfully aware of the stories of Christian young people turning away from their faith as they've progressed into one of these "culture-shaping" careers. Rather than becoming roaring lambs, they were led astray like mere sheep. Do I really believe it is wise to send a young girl to Hollywood to pursue her dream of becoming an actress? If your son has a gift for painting, should he move to New York City and try to make it as an artist?

If we really hope to reclaim these very important fields for God, we have no choice. Hollywood will not clean itself up. It needs Christians who will support decent movies, but it also needs Christian actors, actresses, and filmmakers who will help make good movies. Sure it's a risk. Your kids will face one of the toughest environments in which to live out their faith, but if they are good, they will make it. And if the church surrounded them, prayed for them, supported them, loved them, and stood by them, they will most likely hold onto their faith in Christ.

I recall numerous missionary conventions where young people would be challenged to commit themselves to missions. Often at the close of those conventions young people would stream to the front of the sanctuary, publicly acknowledging the call of God to become missionaries. There were often tears—parents weeping at the prospect of their sons and daughters going off to dangerous lands hostile to the Gospel. The speaker would warn them that it wouldn't be easy; that they might even give their lives as martyrs. But it would be worth it because the lost would be introduced to Jesus.

That same spirit needs to prevail when we think about sending our children into the rough and tumble world of television, film, and other culture-shaping careers. These are the new missionaries that have a shot at turning our nation back toward God. I envision a whole new generation of roaring lambs who will lay claim to these careers with the same vigor and commitment that sent men like Hudson Taylor to China. Will you dare share that vision with me?

In the preface of this book, I tried to relay something of my questions about the purpose for many of the things I have been allowed to do. In no way do I have all the answers. I have not arrived. God has helped me, however, to see and understand something of what He wants me to do. He wants me to study and obey His Word. I know He wants me to be salt. The Word tells me so. I want also to be a lamb that roars for Him in such a way that the sound becomes light, illuminating the Cross and directing men and women to the One who died there. He commands us all to do this. He gives us the privilege of doing this and to be in the arena, in the game—the one that counts for eternity.

Don't sit on the bench. Roar into action. Throw your head back, shake your mane, and really roar for Christ! The rewards are incalculable, beyond price.

study guide

In Roaring Lambs I've stressed the need for Christians to do more than criticize and decry evil. We need to replace the evil with something better. Throughout the book I've suggested ways to do this. Now I'd like to offer some discussion questions and prescribe specific steps that practically anyone can try. After you have worked through the questions and read the action steps, take the Roaring Lambs Voice Test on page 11. If your score isn't where you'd like it, go back and select just five action steps you can include in your daily life. Before long, you'll find your voice and roar like a lion.

chapter 1

Discussion Questions

1. Why is shaping culture such an important part of being salt and light in today's world?

2. Do you agree that the church has little, if any, impact on culture? Can you think of Christians in America or in your community who are making an impact on the media, the arts, or education?

3. In what ways is the Christian subculture a ghetto? Why have we been fooled into thinking we're important?

4. "Real people with real problems" don't care about the things we Christians find important. What are the things your non-Christian neighbors care about? (Are you having trouble answering this question? If so, why?)

5. What are the dangers of "sectioning" our lives—being Christians on Sunday and living like everyone else the rest of the week?

6. Why is it we think that the worst thing we could do is invite our unsaved friends to church or witness to them? Isn't this our scriptural mandate?

   Read Matthew 28:19–20; Mark 16:15; and 1 Corinthians 9:19–23. How can we lead others to Christ by doing well in our jobs? Are we then condoning their belief that job success is paramount?

7. Our pessimistic vision has kept the church from having a greater impact on the culture. What other excuses do Christians typically give for our lack of involvement?

8. For what reasons have Christians historically been reluctant to take part in the media, literature, music, and art? Are there some areas of popular culture that are inherently unchristian?

   In what ways have we defined and carried out the command to be "in the world but not of it"?

9. Measure the impact your church is having on your community. Are you comfortable with this amount of involvement? Do you think it's possible to have a greater impact?

Action Steps

1. Write down the names of three high-school- or college-age young people you know personally. If you have children in this age group, they should be on your list.

2. Try to meet with each individual socially (or call or write them) and let them know you are interested in what they plan to do in life, what careers they might be planning, where they hope to be in ten years. If these are not your own children, develop a relationship with them. Maybe you need to do this, too, if they *are* your own children.

3. Tell them you believe they could help change the world and that you will be praying for them regularly to become "roaring lambs." Help them see that any career is an opportunity to influence the world with the Gospel.

4. Follow through by praying specifically for each of these young people. Pray that God will use them to change the world for His sake.

5. Consider yourself a "career coach" to these young people by encouraging them to aim high. Be the one person who believes in their "naïve" dreams.

6. Give each of these individuals a copy of this book!

Chapter 2

Discussion Questions

1. What does "salt" mean to you? In what ways have you tried to be salty thus far in your Christian life?

2. A year ago, whom would you have considered the "saltiest" Christian you know? Why? What about now? Has your opinion changed?

3. In what ways can Christians add flavor to the world? In what ways can we cleanse and preserve?

4. What professions and areas of interest do you consider the furthermost from being Christian? Are any of them too corrupt for Christians to enter?

5. Consider the ways in which Christians have participated in the entertainment and journalistic media, the arts, and literature—if not in the public arena, then at least within the Christian subculture. In what ways might the other current culture have influenced the church's involvement? Do you think Christians tend to mirror the world around them or "do their own thing"?

6. Read 2 Corinthians 6:14–18 and Colossians 3:1–3. Is it possible for a Christian to be successful in a profession without compromising his or her Christian values or giving the wrong impression? Are Christians ever justified in separating themselves from the world?

7. In your opinion, are protests, boycotts, and petitions really as ineffective as claimed in *Roaring Lambs*? What has the church gained through these methods? What has the church lost?

8. In *Roaring Lambs* I cite these negative actions as signs of a "scorekeeping mentality." In what other ways are Christians today being scorekeepers? What is wrong with this way of thinking? Do Christians have a right to a more Christian world?

9. The church's mission "is not to take over the various communities in our world," but isn't this just what Christians today are trying to do? Consider the last presidential election. Where were the most outspoken Christians in politics and what were their agendas? What were their attitudes toward the result of the election? Does power have a place in Christianity?

10. Make a list of the gripes you have about your local TV and movie offerings, art displays in your community, your schools and school board, and so on. Then, next to each gripe, list a positive action you can take to better the situation.

11. Examine your church's evangelism and discipleship-training programs. What do these programs train people to do? Do they take the trainees' occupations and skills into consideration? Or are they strictly church-related?

12. How can your church support young people as they prepare for careers? Consider starting a mentoring program, matching each college student with an adult in your congregation who works in a similar field, or make up a list of adults willing to be prayer partners with young people.

Action Steps

1. Rent a movie and watch it with your spouse or a close friend. After it's over, list ways it might have been made differently had it been produced and directed by a committed Christian.

2. Watch a popular television program during prime time. Afterward, list ways it might have been different had it been produced and directed by Christians. Would it have been as funny? As moving? As suspenseful? Why or why not?

3. Read your local newspaper for one week and keep track of every reference to religion. Does your paper's treatment of religion reflect the role of religion in your community? If not, consider one or more of the following steps:

   a. Write a friendly letter to the editor (not for publication) expressing your concerns and inviting him to visit your church next Sunday.

   b. Seek an appointment with the editor, religion reporter, or staff reporter simply to talk about the paper's philosophy of covering religion.

   c. Ask your pastor if the church has a person or committee devoted to communicating news of the church to the local paper. If your church doesn't have anyone doing this, urge the pastor to find someone.

   d. Take a collection among your friends to pay for a regular, attractive advertisement to be placed in your paper.

4. Volunteer to form a "roaring lambs club" in your church to meet regularly to discuss ways your church can become more of a force for good in your community and beyond.

Chapter 3

Discussion Questions

1. Who does speak for Christians in America today? Make a list of those Christians you think are most influential in the world.

2. Why can we not leave it all to a spokesperson? Why is every Christian needed to provide salt in today's world?

3. Think of a recent situation you encountered in which Christianity was misunderstood. It may have been in the newspaper, at a public meeting, in a conversation, or whatever. What might you have done or said to set the record straight?

4. Where do equippers fit in the roaring lambs scenario? Who are the equippers in the church today? Are all those in professional Christian ministry equippers? What do you think would be the ideal ratio between equippers and roaring lambs? Or should each Christian be involved in both?

5. In *Roaring Lambs* I criticize a fellow alumnus for not using his talents in a more open, obvious way. Must every Christian be outspoken and participate in public arenas? Read Matthew 5:13–16; 1 Timothy 2:15; and 1 Corinthians 12:14–27.

6. Why do Christians try to make an impact on culture—because we care about bringing the world to Christ or because we want the world to be a more comfortable place for us to live in? Are both motives appropriate for the church's mission?

7. Christians are underrepresented and ignored in public policy while special-interest groups are respected and heeded. What are the characteristics of a special-interest group? What is its primary concern—demanding rights or carrying out responsibilities? Are Christians just another special-interest group? How can we show that we are radically different and still strive to be heard and respected?

8. How can the average Christian develop clout in his or her professional and community life? How can you earn the right to be heard in your area of specialization?

9. Does anyone in your church regularly attend city council or school board meetings—events where public-policy decisions are made? If so, ask these persons to speak to your adult Sunday-school classes about current issues, the state of the council, and other issues of interest. Encourage members to begin attending meetings and become educated about these issues so that they may eventually earn the right to be heard.

Action Steps

1. Write a letter to the editor (for publication) of your local newspaper about an important local issue.

2. Identify one policy-making group in your area and try to attend regularly (school board, city council, zoning board, and so forth).

3. Make a list of everyone in your church who has expertise in a certain area (doctor, lawyer, history teacher, youth worker, auto mechanic, and so forth). Send this list to your local newspaper editor telling him or her that these are resource people who could be contacted by a reporter needing expert information or a public comment about a story dealing with these areas. Note: Include only those individuals who can articulate an opinion or explain something clearly and correctly.

4. Make sure that your church is officially represented at as many public functions as possible. View these "PR" functions as ministry. For starters: parades, county fairs, weekend festivals, hearings, job "expos," and so forth.

5. Sponsor a Christian-artist series or lecture series—events open to the public that showcase the best in Christian entertainment and/or thinking. Advertise these heavily in the community.

Chapter 4

Discussion Questions

1. On page 76, read again the list of values found laudable in old movies. Should movies today be promoting the same values? Were the "good old days" on the silver screen all good and today's movies nearly all bad, considering how old movies portrayed blacks and American Indians, women, war, and physical and mental disabilities? In what ways have movies improved in their communication of values?

2. Who is making today's Christian movies? Where are they shown? What are their purposes?

3. What other high-quality, pro-religion movies have you seen and can add to the *Roaring Lambs'* list?

4. In *Roaring Lambs* I point out that anti-Christian movies typically lose money and pro-religion movies, like *Chariots of Fire*, are big hits. But what about the thousands of movies that are neither anti- nor pro-Christian and are blockbusters because they're high quality? Consider the impact of *Star Wars*, *Indiana Jones*, and *Jurassic Par*k. How much effect do you think religious content, either pro or con, has on the box-office success of a movie? What should be the ultimate test of the success of a pro-Christian film?

5. Make a list of the movies you have seen and videos rented over the past few weeks.
   a. Which ones did you most enjoy? Why?
   b. Did any make you uncomfortable? Why?
   c. In your opinion, what characterizes a good, high-quality movie?

6. What should be the ultimate standards for judging the value content of a film? Should Christian filmmakers avoid foul language, sex and sexual innuendo, and violence? Or

are sex and violence okay if they help develop a moral truth? Compare *Indecent Proposal*, a film loaded with sex that ultimately promotes marital fidelity, with *Sleepless in Seattle*, a relatively clean movie with a simplistic, fairy-tale view of romantic love.

7. Is there a place for films that are morally clean but have no gospel message? Do you think Christian filmmakers should bother with this kind of movie? Are morally sound movies as "salty" as pro-Christian movies?

8. From what you've heard or experienced about the Hollywood movie industry, do you think it's easy to make a pro-Christian movie? What advice would you give to a Christian friend who wants to produce a movie?

9. If you have a young person in your congregation who is interested in screenwriting or movie production, consider sending a "missionary" to Hollywood. Your church may be able to contribute toward living expenses while the person is struggling to get his or her project off the ground.

10. Discuss the movie-rating system with your children. Make sure you know what your specific objections are to each movie they ask about. Help them to make educated decisions and choose movies wisely, despite what all their friends are seeing.

Action Steps

1. Write the Los Angeles Film Studies Center (915 North Cordova Street, Burbank, CA 91505) and ask for information about their program for college students.

2. Whenever a G-rated or other wholesome, family film arrives at local theaters, attend with your family. Make a point to thank the theater manager for scheduling such films.

3. Volunteer to write movie reviews for your local newspaper. Remember, smaller weekly newspapers often use unsolicited material and may be the best place to offer your services.

4. Sponsor a "family movie night" at your church. Rent a quality family film and invite families from your neighborhood. Advertise in your local paper. Do everything you can to stimulate interest in wholesome films.

5. Form your own local "film advisory board" by asking fellow church members to help you create a list of wholesome, entertaining films that are suitable for family viewing. Update and circulate this list occasionally.

6. Personally resolve to avoid attending movies that are excessive in gratuitous sex and violence. Make this decision by yourself, then stick to it.

Chapter 5

Discussion Questions

1. Why did Christians fifty years ago see TV as inherently evil? If you or someone you know remembers the inception of television, make a list of what people said about it at the time. Are the comments similar to those directed at rock 'n' roll in the 1950s and long hair in the 1960s? Do you see any truth in the anti-TV comments?

2. Why are protests and boycotts not taken seriously by the television industry?

3. Is there a way that Christians can object to offensive programming without being accused of censorship?

4. Why are protests and boycotts the "easy way out"? Should Christians stop these efforts entirely? How might Donald Wildmon change his group's tactics to include some positive efforts toward bettering television?

5. Jewish characters are usually presented with integrity and sympathy, while Protestant characters are either nonexistent or portrayed as flakes. Yet the Jewish characters mentioned seldom, if ever, talk about or demonstrate their faith. In fact, Joel Fleischman on *Northern Exposure* has denied the existence of God. These characters are Jews in culture only. How important is cultural uniqueness in the portrayal of religious characters on TV? Do you think TV producers would be less reluctant to include programs about an Amish family or the black church than programs about white, middle-class Protestants?

6. What are the Christian church's great stories? What would you like to see on TV?

7. A successful program must have the "strong, measurable potential to draw a large audience." What do you think are the criteria for measuring this potential? What do you think most viewers want in a TV program?

8. If you haven't already done so, become a member of your local public television station (with as large a donation as possible). When the station runs a pro-religious program, write thank-you letters to the program director or the editor of the station's program guide.

9. What can you do to refute the belief that Christians don't watch quality television? Encourage people in your church to examine their viewing by running reviews in the church newsletter, hosting a small-group "TV night" when a good program is on, or providing a parent workshop in monitoring children's TV watching.

10. At the beginning of each week, look through the TV-viewing guide with your family and decide what shows you will watch. Talk about why the good programs are good and the bad programs bad. Make sure the TV is on only during the chosen good programs.

Action Steps

1. The next time you watch a television program that supports or even enhances your Christian values, write a letter of thanks to the major advertisers (write down the companies advertising and look for their addresses on their products—sometimes you'll even find toll-free numbers listed. If so, call and say thanks).

2. Become a volunteer at your local public-access cable television station. By law, every local cable company has to devote time and facilities to local cable production. You will be trained in how to produce your own programming and can develop programs for the public-access channel.

3. Identify young people in your church who are interested in television (which includes almost all of them). With your youth pastor's help, challenge them to pursue careers in writing for television.

4. Volunteer to write reviews of television programs for your local paper.

5. Invite a local television "celebrity" or program manager to come and talk with your congregation about television. Make it a "get-to-know-each-other" session rather than a chance to complain about lousy TV.

6. Ask your pastor to consider having the church become a corporate sponsor of your local public television station. Encourage others to become volunteers at the station. Remember, becoming a "roaring lamb" is as much about presence (being there) as it is about producing (hands-on television work).

Chapter 6

Discussion Questions

1. Chapter 3 discusses equippers. What percentage of Christian literature do you estimate is important for equipping believers? What percentage would have been better aimed at the current culture?

2. John Grisham is cited as a "roaring lamb." Is it okay for Christian writers to write books that involve violence, foul language, and sexual references but end with good prevailing over evil? Is there any merit in books that are clean and moral but open-ended?

3. What does the new trend in co-publishing say about how non-Christian publishers view the church and Christian literature?

4. What themes do you think Christian writers should be addressing in books aimed at the culture? Consider the interests and needs of your non-Christian family members and friends.

5. Most Christian colleges offer degrees or degree emphases in writing. Many of these colleges have strong ties with Christian publishers, providing field trips and internships, but few have ties with other publishers. How might Christian colleges establish contact with publishers in the world?

6. What genre of Christian books do you usually read? What genre of books do you prefer? If your favorite kind of book were available by a Christian author, would you read it? Do you think it would be as good? Why or why not?

7. What percentage of the magazines you subscribe to or read regularly is Christian-oriented? What percentage is Christian? If the ratio is not 50/50, what magazines might

you begin reading in order to broaden your knowledge of the mainstream culture?

8. Do you think it a sound principle that Christian writers should tithe their time to popular writing? What kind of book would you like to see your favorite Christian writer produce? If you work for a Christian organization or in a Christian field, how might you (and those you work with) benefit from adopting the time-tithing principle?

9. Make a list of books you have read that are written by Christians or deal with pro-religious themes. Buy copies for your church library and review them in your church newsletter.

Action Steps

1. For every Christian book you read, read one from a secular publisher.

2. Visit your local Christian bookstore and ask the manager to consider stocking good, decent, affirming books from secular publishers.

3. Visit your favorite local secular bookstore and ask the manager to consider stocking more religious books. Tell him or her you would visit the store more frequently if you thought you could find Christian books there.

4. Volunteer to write book reviews for your local paper.

5. Ask your local paper to review Christian books now and then.

6. If you notice that your son or daughter enjoys writing, talk with him or her about a writing career, offering encouragement to explore possibilities in secular publishing.

Chapter 7

Discussion Questions

1. What is Christian art? Visit your local Christian bookstore and observe the artwork on the walls. Ask the clerk to show you books that contain Christian art. What styles do you see? What themes are most often portrayed? How do these works of art compare with what you might see in a gallery or museum?

2. Why are so many Christians art-illiterate? What part do the visual arts play in mainstream American culture? How has the church typically responded to the various artistic philosophies and methods over the past three centuries? What do you think we are most afraid of in the visual arts?

3. Do you think American Christians would really appreciate quality Christian art if they saw it? How many people in your church consider themselves art-aware?

4. I contend that those of us closest to the Creator are actually the least creative. What role does imagination play in your spiritual life? In your worship? In the Christian education of your children? Do you think Christians should limit the use of imagination? Why or why not?

5. In *Roaring Lambs* I bemoan the lack of "quality art that depicts biblical themes." Must all Christian art depict Christ, church buildings, worship, or biblical events? Consider the works of art you have seen that fall somewhere between Bible art and Mapplethorpe. Did the majority of these works leave you feeling uplifted? Did they make you think and help you see something a new way? Or did the majority of the works leave you feeling soiled or wanting to get away?

6. I'd love to see a "Christian Ansel Adams." If you are familiar with the work of photographer Ansel Adams, do you

consider his work unchristian? Why or why not? What artistic themes and styles do you find most compatible with Christianity? What artistic themes and styles, if any, do you feel are incompatible with Christianity?

7. If you could commission a work of art that would represent the church to the world, what theme(s) would it depict? What medium would you use? Where would you display it?

8. Visit an art museum or gallery with your family. Which works do you think portray pro-Christian themes? Which works express truth?

9. If you have the opportunity, visit the art department of a large Christian college. What kinds of art are on display there? What are the professors producing? Where are their works displayed? Who are the most successful artists among the alumni?

10. Write to Christians in the Visual Arts; ask for a list of members in your area and, if possible, places and publications in which their works are displayed. Familiarize yourself with the most prominent Christian artists and their work. If you are financially able, begin collecting the work of a Christian artist you especially like.

Action Steps

1. Visit an art museum or exhibit. Take your children with you. Have each family member select a favorite work of art and explain why he or she likes it. If you truly enjoyed your visit, write a letter of thanks to the curator, explaining that you are a Christian and appreciate good art.

2. Visit your local public library and check out books of art prints and quality photography. Have them available for your children to browse. As a family project, study and get to know one serious artist.

3. If you have any children who seem to be gifted in drawing or painting, encourage them. Frame one of their drawings and display it in your home. Encourage them to enter contests.

4. Consider forming a committee at your church to sponsor a fine-arts exhibit.

5. Talk with your pastor about supporting a Christian artist. This could be a one-time grant or a regular stipend.

6. Propose to your church governing body that money be set aside each year to commission a piece of art to be displayed in the church.

Chapter 8

Discussion Questions

1. What reasons do students and their parents typically give for choosing a Christian college over a public one? What can a Christian college offer that a public college or university can't?

2. Why are Christian colleges not producing "roaring lambs"? Why are confidence and vision so important? What might a student be able to achieve if given confidence and vision in addition to commitment and ideals?

3. If you are a Christian college alumnus/alumna, what was the emphasis at your school: learning or ministry? How well prepared were you to enter the working world?

4. Do you think Christian colleges would do a better job of turning out "roaring lambs" if they had more moneys? Ask yourself these questions about your Christian college or one your son or daughter may be considering. (The college catalog may have the information.)

   a. What percentage of the faculty has degrees from public universities?

    b. With what organizations or corporations are adjunct faculty affiliated?

    c. What percentage of alumni works in not-specifically-Christian fields?

    d. What percentage of those on the board of directors work in public fields?

5. What qualities do you think a "roaring lambs" college should have? If you were a professor of your field of expertise, what would you hope to communicate to your students that would help them to make an impact on the societal culture?

6. How can the church help students who choose to attend public institutions? Can these young people also have an opportunity to become "roaring lambs"?

7. Call your local university or community college and find out which campus-ministry groups are active there: InterVarsity Fellowship, Campus Crusade, Young Life, and so on. Consider helping out with one of these ministries or training someone from your church to help out.

8. If you own a business or work for a public company, consider offering internships for Christian college students.

Action Steps

1. Write the Christian College Coalition and request a copy of *Choose a Christian College*. Ask to be put on their mailing list. Address: Christian College Coalition, 329 Eighth Street, N.E., Washington, D.C. 20002.

2. Ask your pastor if your denomination or church is affiliated with a Christian college. If so, request copies of the college catalog and "view book" (promotional brochure describing the school). Consider visiting the campus.

3. Propose to your church's governing board that the congregation "adopt" a Christian college and provide financial support as well as prospective students.

4. Invite a representative of a nearby Christian college to visit your church to talk with the young people about Christian higher education.

5. Volunteer to take a group of young people to a concert or sporting event at a nearby Christian college.

6. If you are a graduate of a Christian college, become active in your alumni association. Attend homecoming activities. Get to know the students. Take an active interest in the school. Use whatever influence you have to promote excellence as a goal for your alma mater.

7. Become a mentor or "pen pal" to one student at a Christian college. Ideally, you will choose a student majoring in a field in which you have expertise and professional knowledge (contact the academic dean's office and ask for names of a few students majoring in _____). Write or call with encouragement. Send a care package now and then. Offer career advice. If possible, provide job leads as graduation approaches. Help this young man or woman become a roaring lamb.

8. If you have influence over the hiring of new personnel at your place of business, seek out candidates from Christian colleges as well as from public schools.

9. Pray regularly for all Christian colleges.

Chapter 9

Discussion Questions

1. Throughout *Roaring Lambs,* I urge Christians to contribute to the media, the arts, and literature through high-quality,

well-planned visual and written works. In your opinion, are most American Christians today amply in touch with the world and able to integrate their personal and church lives well enough to have an impact on the prevailing culture? If you had the opportunity right now, would you feel able to produce something that would positively affect your community? Why or why not?

2. More church money should be given to work in the media, arts, and literature. Where is this money going to come from? What percentage of the missions budget do you think should be allotted for "roaring lambs" ministries? If your church would call for an "over-and-above" offering for, say, producing a feature film, what do you think the response would be?

3. Christians should be supporting the good things and refusing to support the bad. Given the fact that no two Christians will completely agree on what's good and what's bad, do you think we can pull together enough to make an impact on the current culture? How can the Christians in your congregation work together despite disagreements?

4. In *Roaring Lambs* I state, "You can *do* Christianity as well as *be* a Christian." As Christians, where is our identity found? As we are doing our best in our jobs or planning and implementing culture-shaping projects, what must our priorities be?

5. In addition to movies, TV, books, and the arts, what are some other culture-shaping arenas you have contact with or an interest in? Perhaps you are active in community theater, an orchestra, a dance group, or a band. Perhaps you support public radio, or are active in bringing special assemblies to your elementary school. What can you do to bring a positive atmosphere to these arenas, one in which religion and values are accepted and communicated?

6. Is there a place in the "roaring lambs" scenario for Christians who shape, not culture, but people? Can educators, social workers, counselors, pastors, and others who work directly with people have as much of an impact on the current culture as those in the "Roaring Lambs Hall of Fame"? Why or why not?

7. What opportunities do those who attend your church have for career support and "roaring lambs" training? Small groups for businesspersons, medical professionals, writers, working women, builders and tradespeople, public educators, and so on will provide support and encouragement for those wanting to become "roaring lambs." (But don't forget your discussion of Question #4 above.)

8. Plan a short-term small group around an issue you would like to address: something from the newspaper, a school board issue, TV offerings, a local art exhibit, a political campaign, or whatever. Plan and implement *positive* actions such as writing thank-you letters, newspaper reviews, or sending a representative.

9. Reread the suggestions on pages 173–76 for encouraging and inspiring those in your church to become "roaring lambs." Plan a strategy for proposing action:
   a. To whom will you present your stragegy: the pastor, the board, the Sunday school?
   b. What area of concern will you address: schools, the arts, the media, politics?
   c. What are your suggestions for what the church should do?
   d. What do *you* plan on doing, whether or not anyone joins you?

10. Make a list of community events, TV programs, movies, magazine articles, and so on from the past few weeks that you have appreciated. Write thank-you letters to the

appropriate people. Be sure to involve your children in this activity.

11. Pray that God will guide you to opportunities to become a "roaring lamb."

roaring lambs

the CD release featuring new music from

Jars of Clay
Sixpence None the Richer
Michael W. Smith
Steven Curtis Chapman
Burlap to Cashmere
& more

Available on CD and Cassette from Squint Entertainment

www.squinterland.com

www.roaringlambs.net – log on to nominate the roaring lambs in your life for the Roaring Lambs Hall of Fame

Order Roaring Lambs
The Album from
World Distribution

CD: 080688602925
CS: 080688602949

squint
ENTERTAINMENT

We want to hear from you. Please send your comments about this
book to us in care of the address below. Thank you.

ZondervanPublishingHouse
Grand Rapids, Michigan 49530
http://www.zondervan.com